★★★★★★★★★★ HARCOURT **HORIZONS**

HARCOURT HORIZONS

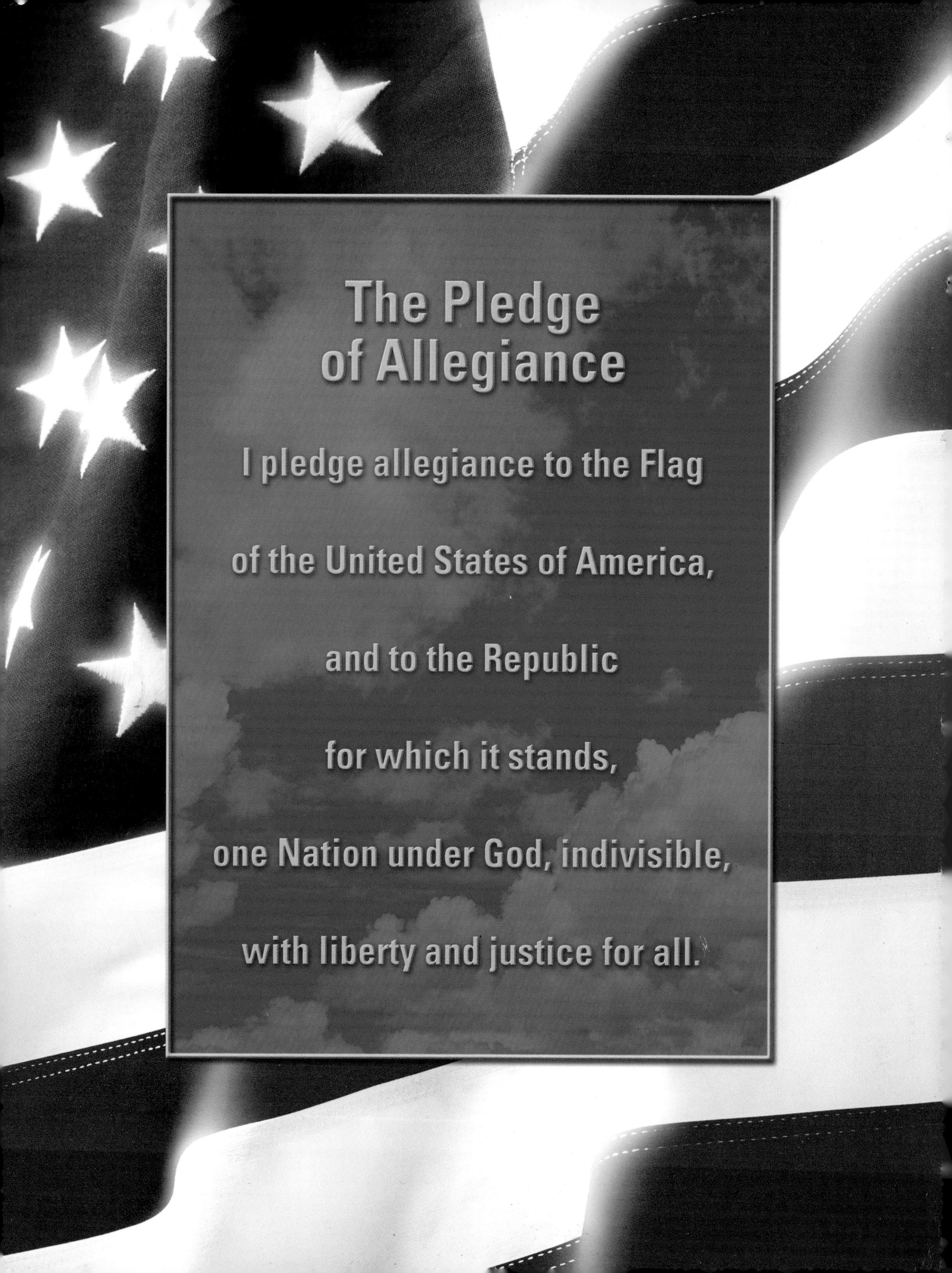

The Pledge of Allegiance

I pledge allegiance to the Flag

of the United States of America,

and to the Republic

for which it stands,

one Nation under God, indivisible,

with liberty and justice for all.

★★★★★★★★★★ **HARCOURT HORIZONS**

About My World

Harcourt

Orlando   Austin   Chicago   New York   Toronto   London   San Diego

Visit *The Learning Site!*
www.harcourtschool.com

HARCOURT HORIZONS

ABOUT MY WORLD

General Editor

Dr. Michael J. Berson
Associate Professor
Social Science Education
University of South Florida
Tampa, Florida

Contributing Authors

Dr. Sherry Field
Associate Professor
The University of Texas at Austin
Austin, Texas

Dr. Tyrone Howard
Assistant Professor
UCLA Graduate School of
   Education & Information Studies
University of California at Los
   Angeles
Los Angeles, California

Dr. Bruce E. Larson
Associate Professor of Teacher
   Education and Social Studies
Western Washington University
Bellingham, Washington

Series Consultants

Dr. Robert Bednarz
Professor
Department of Geography
Texas A&M University
College Station, Texas

Linda McMillan Fields
Social Studies Supervisor
Spring Branch Independent
   School District
Houston, Texas

Dr. Asa Grant Hilliard III
Fuller E. Callaway Professor
   of Urban Education
Georgia State University
Atlanta, Georgia

Dr. Thomas M. McGowan
Chairperson and Professor
Center for Curriculum and
   Instruction
University of Nebraska
Lincoln, Nebraska

Dr. John J. Patrick
Professor of Education
Indiana University
Bloomington, Indiana

Dr. Cinthia Salinas
Assistant Professor
Department of Curriculum and
   Instruction
University of Texas at Austin
Austin, Texas

Dr. Philip VanFossen
Associate Professor,
   Social Studies
   Education, and
   Associate Director,
   Purdue Center for Economic
   Education
Purdue University
West Lafayette, Indiana

Dr. Hallie Kay Yopp
Professor
Department of
   Elementary, Bilingual,
   and Reading Education
California State
   University, Fullerton
Fullerton, California

Maps
researched and prepared by

Readers
written and designed by

Take a Field Trip
video tour segments provided by

Copyright © 2003 by Harcourt, Inc.

Acknowledgments appear in the back of this
book.

Printed in the United States of America

ISBN 0-15-320178-9

5 6 7 8 9 10 032 10 09 08 07 06 05 04

Contents

A1 Atlas

· UNIT ·

1

Going to School

1 Unit 1 Introduction

2 Unit 1 Preview the Vocabulary

4 Start with a Poem
School Bus by Lee Bennett Hopkins
illustrated by Lori Lohstoeter

6 **Lesson 1 Going to School**

8 **Reading Skills**
Find the Main Idea

10 **Lesson 2 Rules at School**

12 **Citizenship Skills**
Working Together

14 **Lesson 3 School Workers**

18 **Lesson 4 Where Are You?**

20 **Map and Globe Skills**
Looking at Maps

22 **Lesson 5 Schools Long Ago and Today**

28 **Chart and Graph Skills**
Put Things into Groups

30 **Lesson 6 Learning Around the World**

34 Visit
A School for Firefighters

36 Unit 1 Review and Test Preparation

40 Unit Activities

· UNIT ·

2

Good Citizens

41 Unit 2 Introduction

42 Unit 2 Preview the Vocabulary

44 Start with a Song
    America by Samuel F. Smith
    illustrated by Erika LeBarre

46 **Lesson 1 Rules and Laws**

48 **Lesson 2 Who Are Our Leaders?**

52 Map and Globe Skills
    Find States on a Map

54 **Lesson 3 Our Country's Presidents**

58 Citizenship Skills
    Make a Choice by Voting

60 **Lesson 4 America's Symbols**

66 Reading Skills
    Fiction or Nonfiction

68 **Lesson 5 Portraits of Good Citizens**

72 **Lesson 6 Rights and Responsibilities**

74 Visit
    How Communities Honor Their Citizens

76 Unit 2 Review and Test Preparation

80 Unit Activities

· UNIT · 3

The Land Around Us

81 Unit 3 Introduction

82 Unit 3 Preview the Vocabulary

84 **Start with a Story**
From Here to There by Margery Cuyler
illustrated by Yu Cha Pak

94 **Lesson 1 A Neighborhood**

96 **Map and Globe Skills**
Use a Map Key

98 **Lesson 2 Land and Water**

102 **Map and Globe Skills**
Find Land and Water on a Map

104 **Lesson 3 Globes and Maps**

106 **Map and Globe Skills**
Find Directions on a Globe

108 **Lesson 4 People and Resources**

112 **Reading Skills**
Predict What Will Happen

114 **Lesson 5 Saving Our Resources**

118 **Lesson 6 Houses and Homes**

122 **Visit**
A Butterfly Garden

124 **Unit 3 Review and Test Preparation**

128 **Unit Activities**

· UNIT ·

4

All About People

129 Unit 4 Introduction

130 Unit 4 Preview the Vocabulary

132 Start with an Article
The Mohawk Way from Time for Kids

134 Lesson 1 People Together

136 Citizenship Skills
Solve a Problem

138 Lesson 2 Families Together

142 Lesson 3 What Is Culture?

146 Reading Skills
Point of View

148 Examine Primary Sources
Expressing Culture

152 Map and Globe Skills
Use a Map Scale

154 Lesson 4 Celebrate!

158 Chart and Graph Skills
Use a Calendar

160 Lesson 5 We Are Americans!

162 Visit
A Festival of Cultures

164 Unit 4 Review and Test Preparation

168 Unit Activities

· UNIT ·

5

Looking Back

169 Unit 5 Introduction

170 Unit 5 Preview the Vocabulary

172 Start with a Poem
Four Generations by Mary Ann Hoberman
illustrated by Russ Wilson

174 **Lesson 1 Time and Change**

176 Chart and Graph Skills
Use a Time Line

178 **Lesson 2 Trace a Family History**

182 Chart and Graph Skills
Use a Diagram

184 **Lesson 3 A Community History**

190 Reading Skills
Identify Cause and Effect

192 **Lesson 4 America's First People**

196 **Lesson 5 Our Country's History**

200 **Lesson 6 Celebrating History**

204 Map and Globe Skills
Follow a Route on a Map

206 **Lesson 7 Parade of Heroes**

210 **Lesson 8 Everyday Life, Past and Present**

216 Examine Primary Sources
The Telephone

218 Visit
Old Sturbridge Village

220 Unit 5 Review and Test Preparation

224 Unit Activities

· UNIT · 6

Jobs People Do

225 Unit 6 Introduction

226 Unit 6 Preview the Vocabulary

228 Start with a Story
Rush Hour by Christine Loomis
illustrated by Mari Takabayashi

240 **Lesson 1 Goods and Services**

244 **Lesson 2 A Pencil Factory**

250 Chart and Graph Skills
Use a Picture Graph

252 **Lesson 3 Why People Work**

254 **Lesson 4 Jobs Change**

258 **Lesson 5 Buyers and Sellers**

262 Chart and Graph Skills
Use a Bar Graph

264 **Lesson 6 Wanting More or Less**

266 Citizenship Skills
Make Choices When Buying

268 **Lesson 7 Trading with Others**

274 Visit
People at Work

276 Unit 6 Review and Test Preparation

280 Unit Activities

Reference

282 Biographical Dictionary

284 Picture Glossary

303 Index

Features You Can Use

Skills

Chart and Graph Skills

28 Put Things into Groups

158 Use a Calendar

176 Use a Time Line

182 Use a Diagram

250 Use a Picture Graph

262 Use a Bar Graph

Citizenship Skills

12 Working Together

58 Make a Choice by Voting

136 Solve a Problem

266 Make Choices When Buying

Map and Globe Skills

20 Looking at Maps

52 Find States on a Map

96 Use a Map Key

102 Find Land and Water on a Map

106 Find Directions on a Globe

152 Use a Map Scale

204 Follow a Route on a Map

Reading Skills

8 Find the Main Idea

66 Fiction or Nonfiction

112 Predict What Will Happen

146 Point of View

190 Identify Cause and Effect

Music and Literature

4 "School Bus"
by Lee Bennett Hopkins
illustrated by Lori Lohstoeter

44 "America"
by Samuel F. Smith
illustrated by Erika LeBarre

84 From Here to There
by Margery Cuyler
illustrated by Yu Cha Pak

132 The Mohawk Way
from Time for Kids

172 "Four Generations"
by Mary Ann Hoberman
illustrated by Russ Wilson

228 Rush Hour
by Christine Loomis
illustrated by Mari Takabayashi

Primary Sources

Examine Primary Sources

148 Expressing Culture

216 The Telephone

American Documents

56 The Constitution of the
United States of America

62 The Pledge of Allegiance

65 The National Anthem

Biography

15 Mary McLeod Bethune

57 Thomas Jefferson

68 Nathan Hale

69 Sam Houston
69 Clara Barton
70 Eleanor Roosevelt
70 Stephanie Kwolek
71 Firefighters
115 Marjory Stoneman Douglas
201 Abraham Lincoln
211 Thomas Alva Edison
257 Ellen Ochoa

Geography

119 Sonoran Desert
249 Graphite from China

Heritage

64 Washington State
156 Kwanzaa

Science and Technology

31 The Internet
181 Clocks

Charts, Graphs, and Diagrams

A12 Geography Terms
1 Comparison Chart
6 Read a Textbook
10 Class Rules
18 Where Are You?
29 School Tools
36 Unit 1 Visual Summary
38 Rules
41 K-W-L Chart
58 Ballot
59 Votes
76 Unit 2 Visual Summary
78 Class Field Trip Votes
81 Geography Web
110 Drilling for Oil
124 Unit 3 Visual Summary
129 Big Idea Web
159 December Calendar
164 Unit 4 Visual Summary
166 October Calendar
169 Sequencing Chart
175 Four Seasons
176 Samuel's Time Line
183 Family Tree
214 Communication Through History
220 Unit 5 Visual Summary
222 Presidents' Birthdays Time Line
225 Summary Web
251 Boxes of Pencils Sold
263 Baskets of Berries Sold
265 Monthly Budget
271 Clothes from Around the World
276 Unit 6 Visual Summary
278 Patients
279 Where Ryan's Shirts Come From

Maps

A2 World Land and Water

A4 World Continents

A6 North America

A8 United States Land and Water

A10 United States

21 School Map

39 Joe's Classroom

53 United States (states)

79 United States

95 Houston Neighborhood

97 Hermann Park

103 Texas

105 World Map

107 Western Hemisphere

107 Eastern Hemisphere

119 Sonoran Desert

126 Western Hemisphere

126 Eastern Hemisphere

127 North Carolina

153 Culture Museum

167 Culture Festival

194 Columbus's Route

205 Veterans Day Parade

223 Bus Routes

249 China

Atlas

 World

A2 Land and Water

A4 Continents

A6 North America

United States

A8 Land and Water

A10 States

Geography Terms

A12

A1

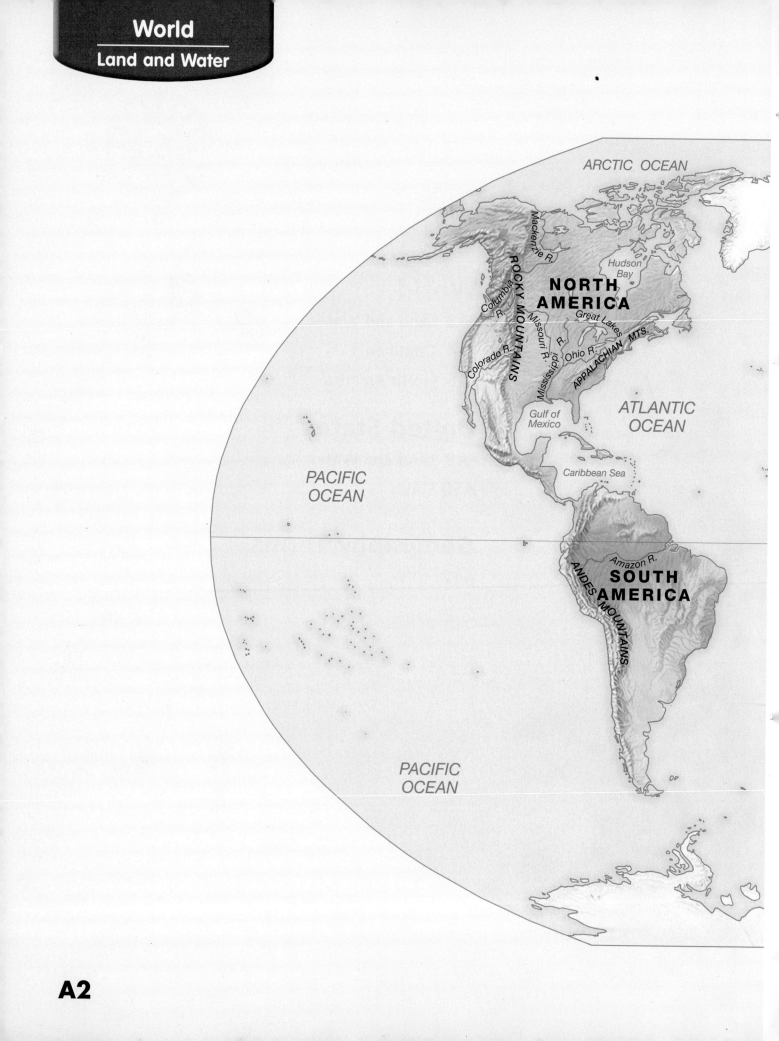

ARCTIC OCEAN

Mackenzie R.

Hudson Bay

ROCKY MOUNTAINS

NORTH AMERICA

Columbia R.

Great Lakes

Missouri R.

Mississippi R.

Ohio R.

APPALACHIAN MTS.

Colorado R.

ATLANTIC OCEAN

Gulf of Mexico

PACIFIC OCEAN

Caribbean Sea

Amazon R.

ANDES MOUNTAINS

SOUTH AMERICA

PACIFIC OCEAN

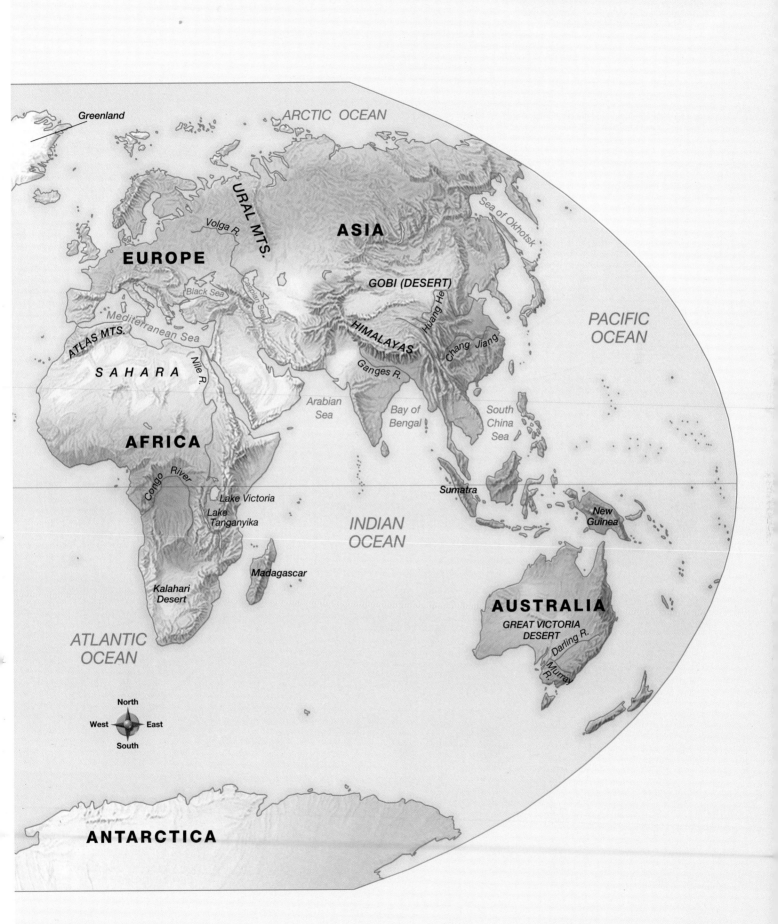

Greenland

ARCTIC OCEAN

URAL MTS.

Volga R.

EUROPE

ASIA

Sea of Okhotsk

Black Sea

Caspian Sea

GOBI (DESERT)

Mediterranean Sea

ATLAS MTS.

HIMALAYAS

Huang He

Chang Jiang

PACIFIC
OCEAN

SAHARA

Nile R.

Ganges R.

Arabian
Sea

Bay of
Bengal

South
China
Sea

AFRICA

Congo River

Lake Victoria

Lake
Tanganyika

Sumatra

INDIAN
OCEAN

New
Guinea

Madagascar

Kalahari
Desert

AUSTRALIA

GREAT VICTORIA
DESERT

Darling R.

ATLANTIC
OCEAN

Murray
R.

North

West   East

South

ANTARCTICA

A3

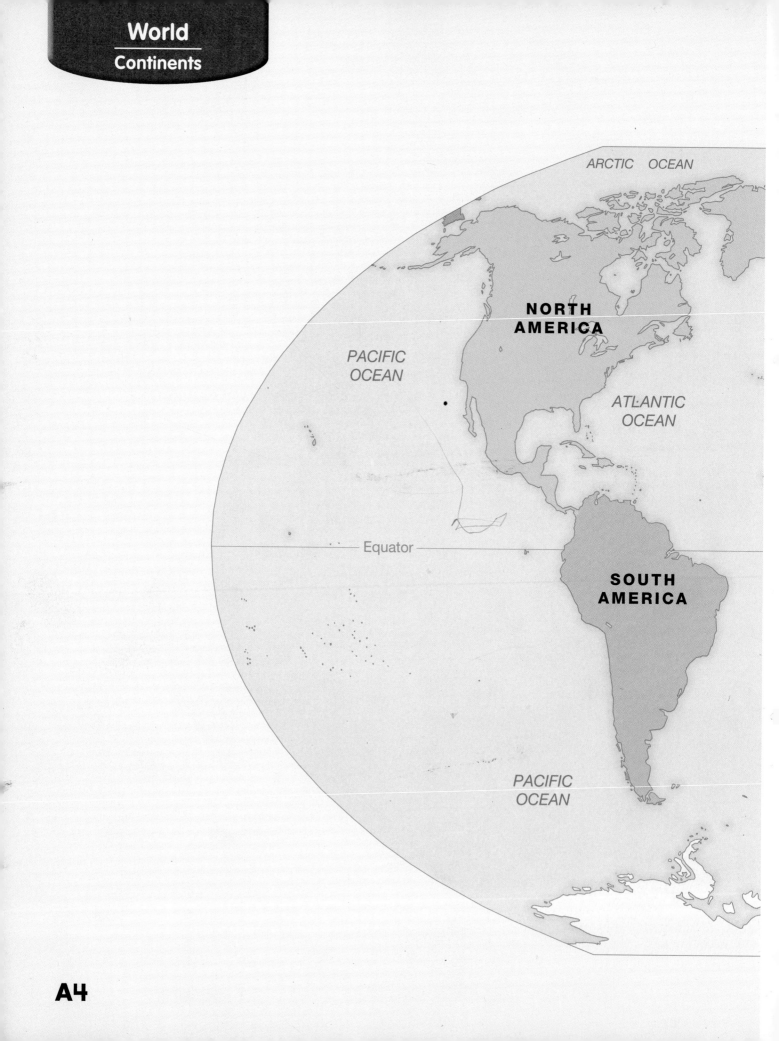

ARCTIC   OCEAN

**NORTH
AMERICA**

*PACIFIC
OCEAN*

*ATLANTIC
OCEAN*

Equator

**SOUTH
AMERICA**

*PACIFIC
OCEAN*

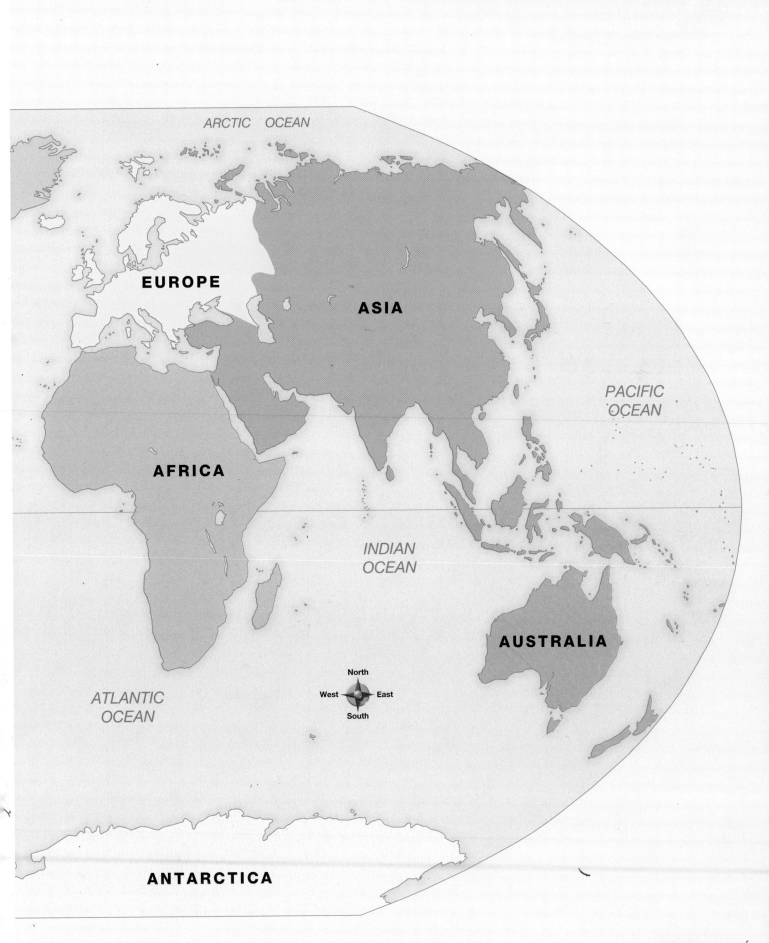

ARCTIC OCEAN

EUROPE

ASIA

PACIFIC OCEAN

AFRICA

INDIAN OCEAN

ATLANTIC OCEAN

AUSTRALIA

North

West — East

South

ANTARCTICA

A5

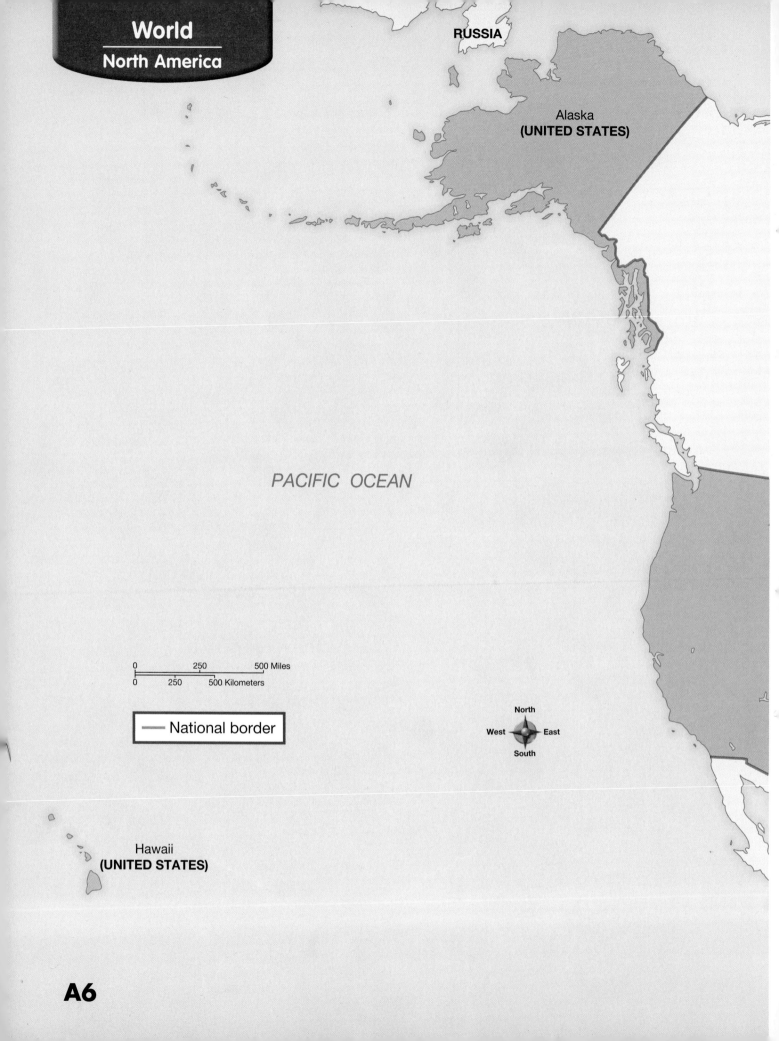

RUSSIA

Alaska
(UNITED STATES)

PACIFIC OCEAN

0   250   500 Miles
0   250   500 Kilometers

—— National border

North
West   East
South

Hawaii
(UNITED STATES)

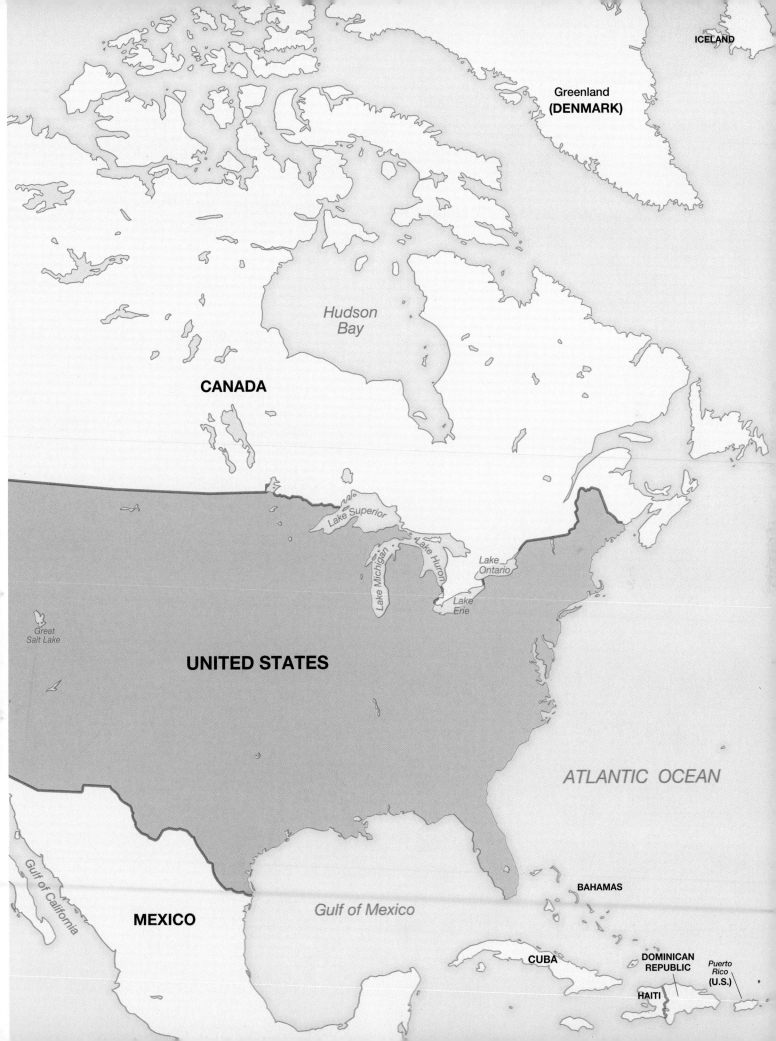

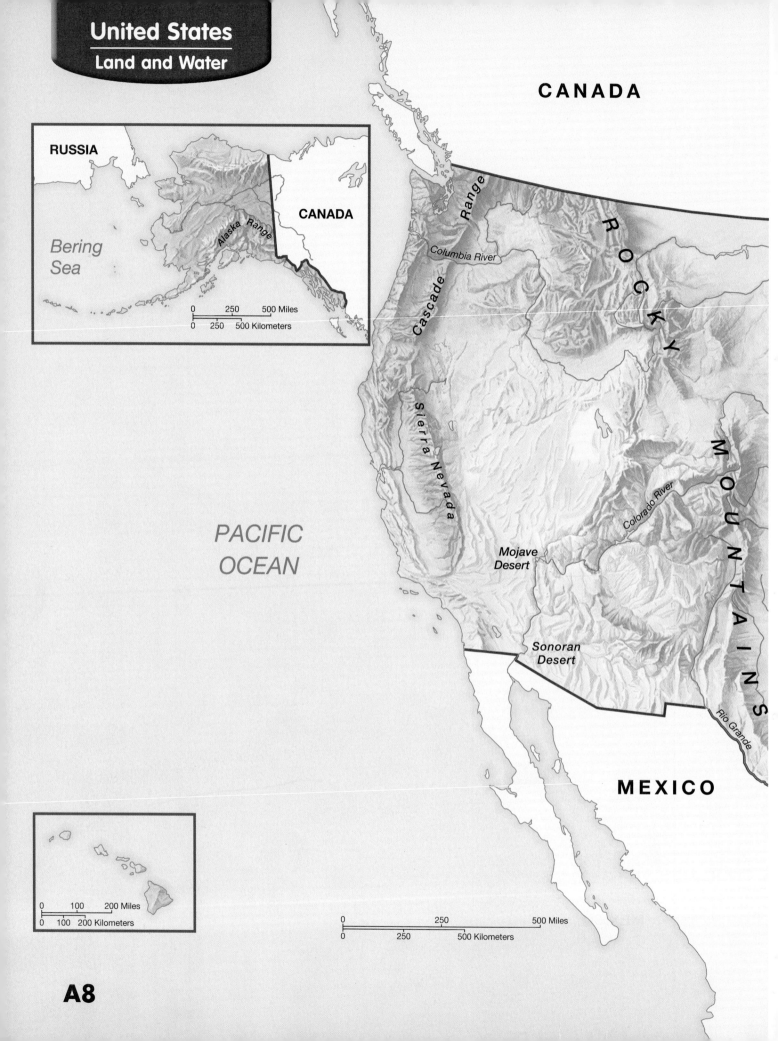

United States
Land and Water

CANADA

RUSSIA

CANADA

Bering Sea

Alaska Range

0   250   500 Miles
0   250   500 Kilometers

R O C K Y

Cascade Range

Columbia River

M O U N T A I N S

PACIFIC OCEAN

Sierra Nevada

Colorado River

Mojave Desert

Sonoran Desert

Rio Grande

MEXICO

0   100   200 Miles
0   100   200 Kilometers

0   250   500 Miles
0   250   500 Kilometers

A8

CANADA

Lake Superior

Lake Huron

Lake Michigan

Lake Ontario

Lake Erie

G R E A T   P L A I N S

Missouri River

Mississippi River

I N T E R I O R
P L A I N S

Missouri River

Ohio River

Mississippi River

A P P A L A C H I A N   M O U N T A I N S

ATLANTIC
OCEAN

C O A S T A L   P L A I N

Rio Grande

BAHAMAS

North
West ⟡ East
South

*Gulf of
Mexico*

Straits of Florida

CUBA

A9

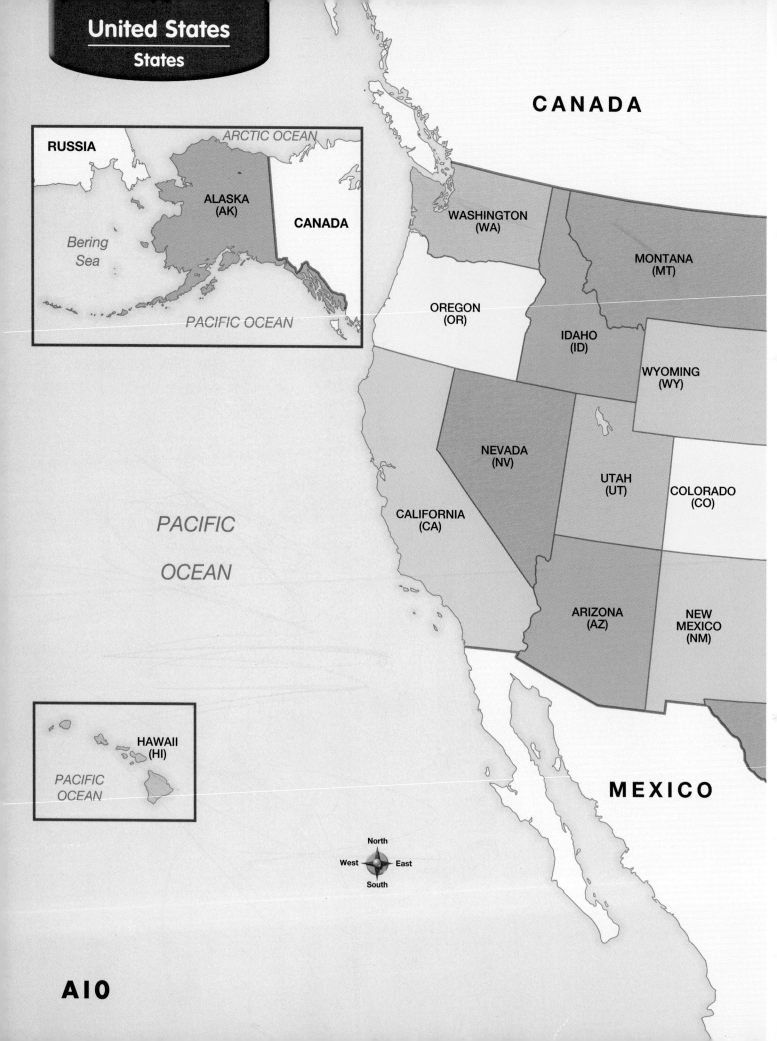

United States
States

CANADA

RUSSIA

ARCTIC OCEAN

ALASKA
(AK)

CANADA

Bering
Sea

PACIFIC OCEAN

WASHINGTON
(WA)

MONTANA
(MT)

OREGON
(OR)

IDAHO
(ID)

WYOMING
(WY)

PACIFIC

OCEAN

NEVADA
(NV)

UTAH
(UT)

COLORADO
(CO)

CALIFORNIA
(CA)

ARIZONA
(AZ)

NEW
MEXICO
(NM)

HAWAII
(HI)

PACIFIC
OCEAN

MEXICO

North

West   East

South

A10

Geography Terms

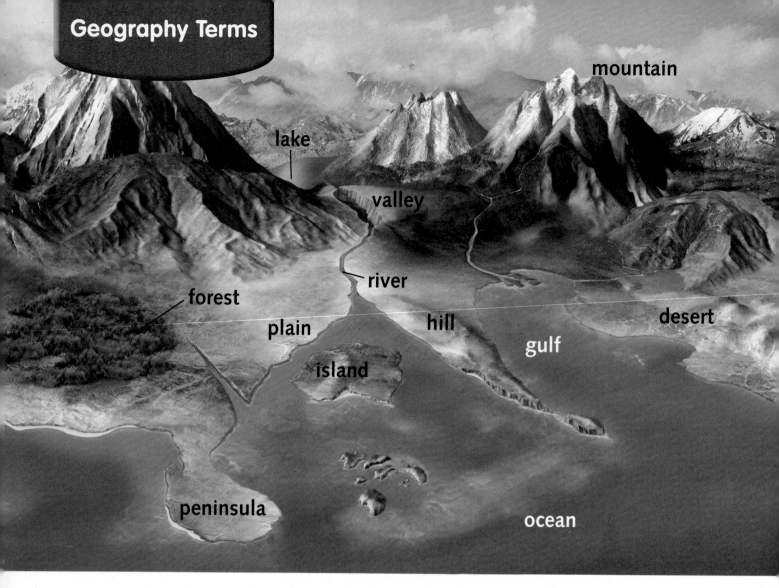

desert a large, dry area of land

forest a large area of trees

gulf a large body of ocean water that is partly surrounded by land

hill land that rises above the land around it

island a landform with water all around it

lake a body of water with land on all sides

mountain highest kind of land

ocean a body of salt water that covers a large area

peninsula a landform that is surrounded on only three sides by water

plain flat land

river a large stream of water that flows across the land

valley low land between hills or mountains

A12

Going to School

Eagle on Uncle Sam's Hat
Tradesign, 1870

Going to School

" Enter to Learn
Depart to Serve **"**

—signs entering and leaving Mary McLeod Bethune's school in Daytona Beach, Florida, 1914

Preview the Content

Make a table to show how schools around the world are alike and different. As you read this unit, add to the table. Show what you learn about school workers, ways you learn, and tools you use.

Schools	
Alike	Different

learn To find out something new. (page 6)

rule An instruction telling what must or must not be done. (page 10)

group A number of people working together. (page 12)

teacher A person who helps others learn. (page 14)

principal The leader of a school. (page 14)

START with a POEM

School Bus

by Lee Bennett Hopkins
illustrated by Lori Lohstoeter

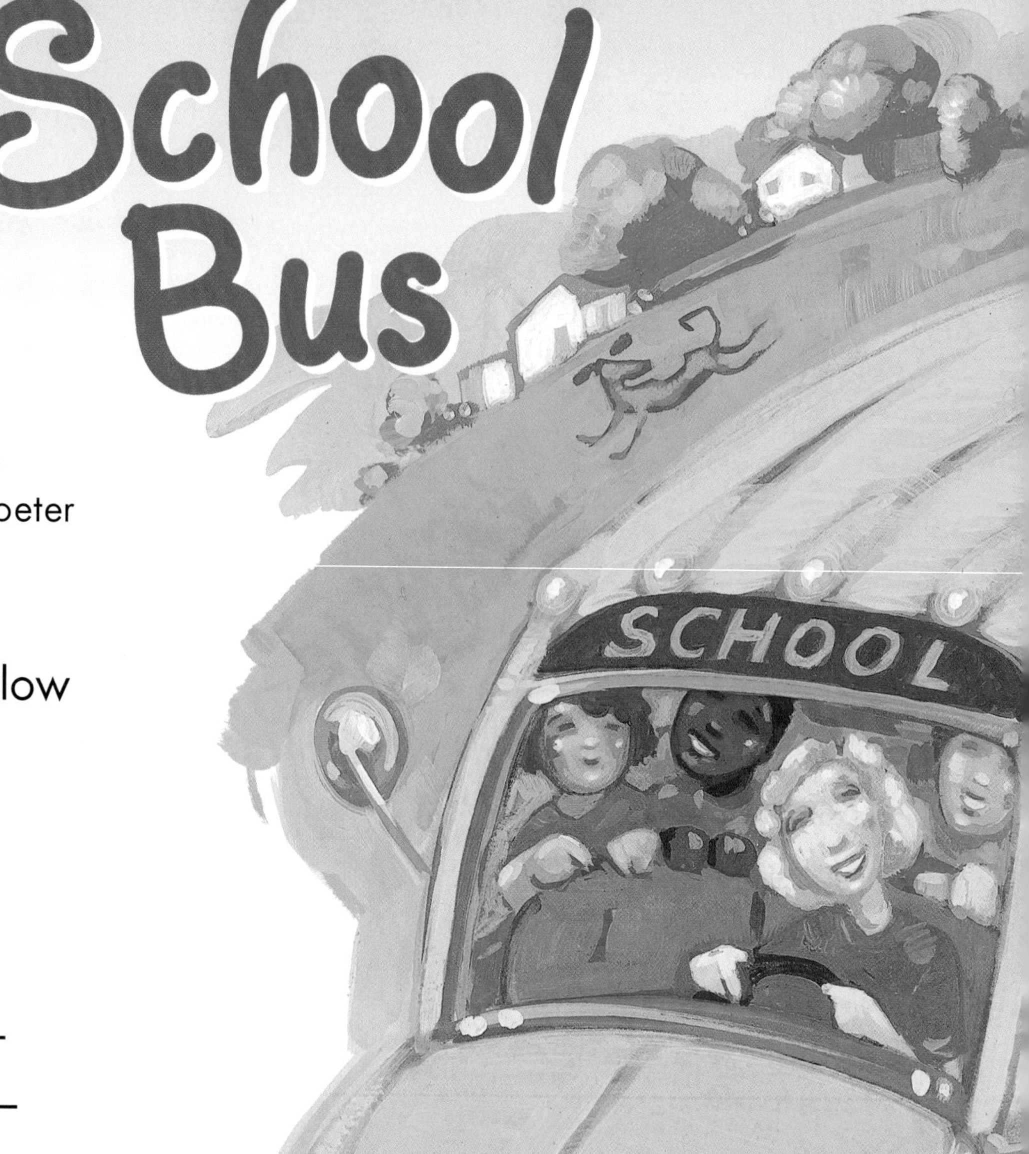

This wide-awake
freshly-painted-yellow
school bus

readied for Fall

carries us all—

Sixteen boys—
Fourteen girls—

Thirty pairs of sleepy eyes

and

hundreds
upon
hundreds

of

school supplies.

Start the Unit Project

A Classroom Scrapbook Your class will start a scrapbook. As you read this unit, draw and write about the new things you learn.

Think About It

1 What does the poem tell you about these children?

2 How do you get ready for school?

Use Technology

 Visit The Learning Site at **www.harcourtschool.com/ socialstudies** for additional activities, primary sources, and other resources to use in this unit.

Lesson

1

Going to School

1. lesson number

2. title

Main Idea
School is a place to learn and share.

Vocabulary

learn

share

Our school is where we learn. When we **learn**, we find out something new. We read at school to learn. We write, draw, and tell stories, too.

3. new word

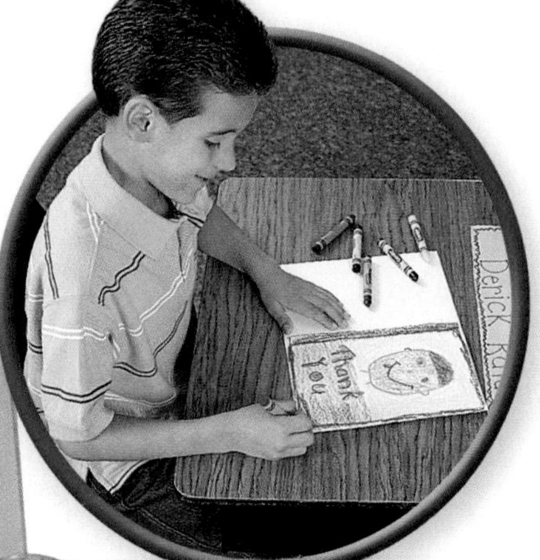

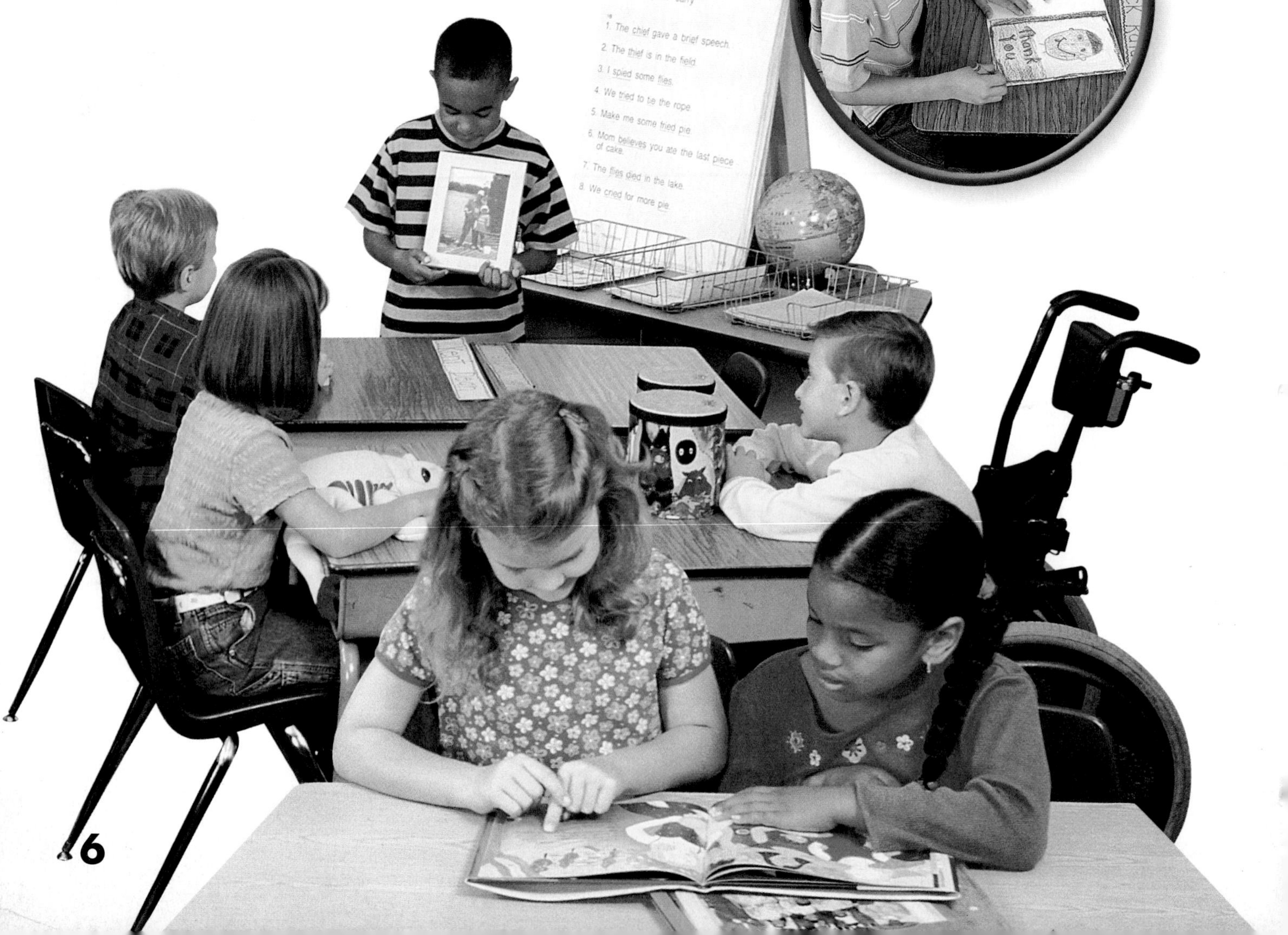

A Classroom Scrapbook   Your class will start a scrapbook. As you read this unit, draw and write about the new things you learn.

Visit The Learning Site at **www.harcourtschool.com/ socialstudies** for additional activities, primary sources, and other resources to use in this unit.

Think About It

1 What does the poem tell you about these children?

2 How do you get ready for school?

1

Going to School

2. title

1. lesson number

Main Idea
School is a place to learn and share.

Vocabulary

learn

share

3. new word

Our school is where we learn. When we **learn**, we find out something new. We read at school to learn. We write, draw, and tell stories, too.

Our school is where we share. We **share** what we know and who we are.

4. picture

5. question

LESSON 1
Review

1. **Vocabulary** What do you want to **learn** in school?

2. What do the pictures tell you about how children in this classroom learn?

3. Draw a picture of something you did today in school.

Find the Main Idea

Vocabulary

main idea

detail

▶ Why It Matters

The **main idea** tells you what you are reading about.

▶ What You Need to Know

A paragraph has a main idea. Paragraphs also have detail sentences. A **detail** gives more information. Details help explain the main idea.

▶ Practice the Skill

1. Read the paragraph on page 9. What is the main idea?

2. What is one detail in the paragraph?

Braille watch

8

Braille

People who cannot see can use the Braille alphabet to read and write. Groups of small, raised dots stand for letters in the alphabet. Other groups of dots stand for numbers. The dot letters spell out words. People who are blind read the words by running their fingers along the dots. ■

▶ Apply What You Learned

Read a children's magazine article. Look for main ideas and details.

Rules at School

Vocabulary

rule

fair

We have rules in our classroom. A **rule** tells what you must do. Rules help us work and play safely.

Class Rules
· Talk quietly.
· Take turns.
· Follow directions.
· Be kind.

Rules help us listen, share, and work together in a fair way. **Fair** means acting in a way that is right and honest.

Follow the rules.

LESSON 2
Review

1 **Vocabulary** How do **rules** help people be **fair**?

2 Explain why we need rules at school.

3 Choose a school rule. Draw a picture of children following that rule.

Working Together

Vocabulary

group

▶ Why It Matters

In school, children may work alone or with others in a **group**. People in a group need to know how to work together.

▶ What You Need to Know

These steps help group members work together.

Step 1 Plan together.

Step 2 Act together.

Step 3 Think about how well your group worked together.

▶ Practice the Skill

① Study the picture.

② Work in a group to write rules the children in this playground can use.

▶ Apply What You Learned

Work with family members to plan an activity. Use the steps you learned.

13

School Workers

Main Idea
There are many workers at a school.

Vocabulary
teacher
principal

Our school has many workers. Our **teacher** helps us learn. Our **principal** helps make our school a safe place.

teacher

principal

• BIOGRAPHY •

Mary McLeod Bethune
1875–1955
Character Trait: Perseverance

When Mary McLeod Bethune was young, there were few schools for African American children. When she found one, she worked hard and became a teacher. She later opened a school and then a college where African Americans could go to learn.

GO ONLINE

MULTIMEDIA BIOGRAPHIES
Visit The Learning Site at
www.harcourtschool.com/biographies
to learn about other famous people.

How are these school workers helping?

nurse

custodian

teacher aide

librarian

food server

LESSON 3
Review

❶ **Vocabulary** How does a **teacher** help children?

❷ How do you help at school?

❸ Make a list of people who help you at school. Write a thank-you card for a worker from your list.

Where Are You?

Main Idea
You can describe a location.

Vocabulary

location

The **location** of a place is where the place is. The drawing shows where the rooms are in this school. Describe the location of each room. Use words such as <u>next to</u>, <u>beside</u>, and <u>across from</u>.

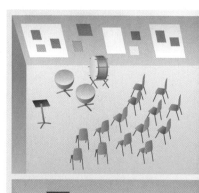

 GEOGRAPHY THEME Which room is between the music room and the gym?

1 **Vocabulary** Describe the **location** of the music room.

2 How is this school like your school?

3 Imagine you are helping a child who is new to your school. Describe the location of rooms he or she might need to find.

Looking at Maps

Vocabulary

map

symbol

▶ Why It Matters

A **map** is a drawing that shows where places are. Maps help you find places.

▶ What You Need to Know

Mapmakers use **symbols**, or pictures, to stand for real things.

playground

music room

cafeteria

gym

classroom

office

library

20

Practice the Skill

1 Look at the map. Where is the playground? How do you know?

2 What rooms are next to the cafeteria?

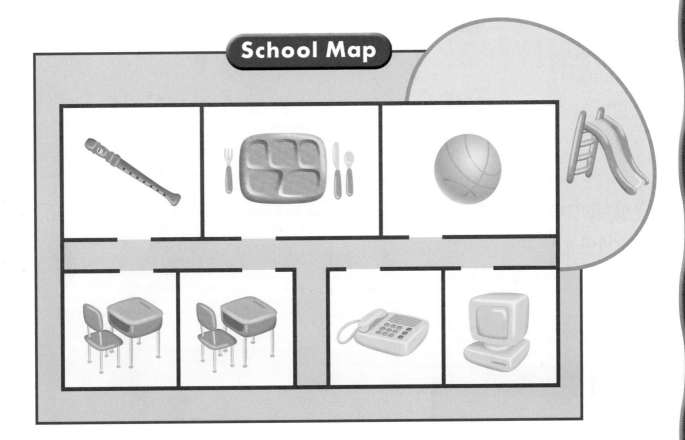

School Map

Apply What You Learned

Make a map of your classroom. Use symbols to show where things are in the room.

 Practice your map and globe skills with the **GeoSkills CD-ROM.**

Main Idea
Schools long ago were like schools today in some ways. They were also different.

Vocabulary

tool

Schools Long Ago and Today

Then

Long ago, some children learned at home. Other children went to one-room schools. There, children of all ages learned together.

Now

Some ways of learning are the same today as they were long ago. Some ways are different. Today there are many more kinds of schools.

Hebrew school

Special-needs school

Home school

Multiage class

23

Then

A **tool** is something people use. Some tools are used for learning. Long ago, children had few tools.

An abacus is a very old tool used for counting. Today most people use a calculator, but some people still use an abacus.

25

Now

Today children use many tools to learn.

❶ **Vocabulary**   What **tools** do you use in school?

❷ How were schools different long ago?

❸ Write three sentences that describe your school.

Put Things into Groups

Vocabulary

table

▶ Why It Matters

Putting things into groups helps you see how they are alike and different.

▶ What You Need to Know

A **table** is a chart that shows things in groups. Labels tell you what is in each group.

▶ Practice the Skill

❶ Look at the chart. Which side shows tools from long ago? Which side shows tools from today?

❷ What did children use to write with long ago? What do they use today?

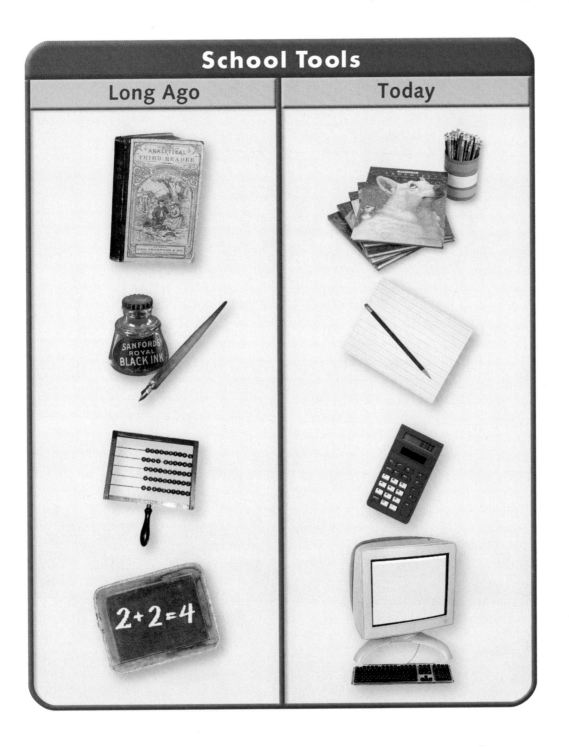

School Tools

Long Ago	Today

▶ Apply What You Learned

Make a table that shows Reading Tools and Writing Tools. Use the tools on the Today side of the table on this page to make your new table.

6

Main Idea
Schools around the world are the same in many ways.

Vocabulary
world

Learning Around the World

The **world** is all the people and places on our planet. Around the world, children learn. Some schools may look like yours, and some may be very different.

Germany

Mexico

The Internet

The Internet makes it easy for people to learn and share. With this tool, you can find information about many things. You can see art in a museum far away. You can even send messages around the world.

Togo

Brazil

31

Some learning
happens outside
of the classroom.
How are these
children learning?

Venezuela

Japan

Egypt

Italy

 LESSON 6
Review

1 Vocabulary What is the **world**?

2 How are the ways these children learn the same as the ways you learn?

3 Write a letter telling someone far away about your school.

A School for Firefighters

Get Ready

There are many kinds of schools. At a school for firefighters, people learn how to fight fires and keep others safe. They also learn how to work together as a team.

What to See

Students help each other use a fire hose.

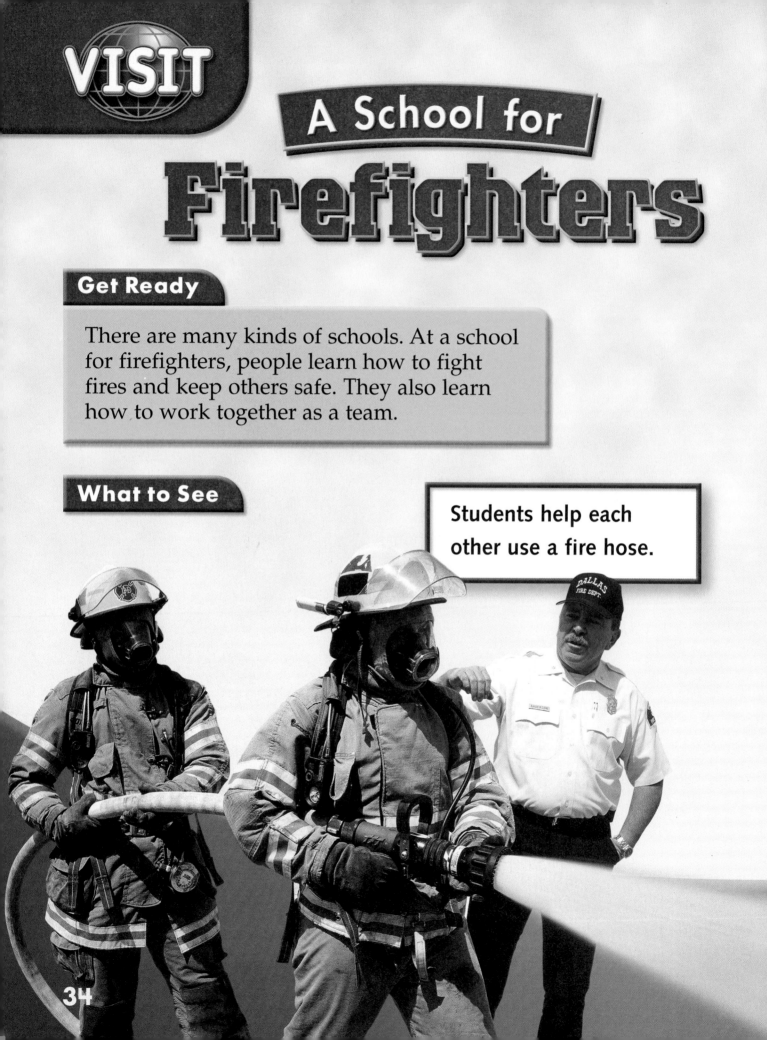

Students practice using a ladder.

There is a lot to learn about the fire truck.

The water hose hooks up to the fire hydrant.

Students study fire safety rules.

Take a Field Trip

A VIRTUAL TOUR
Visit The Learning Site at
www.harcourtschool.com/tours
to take virtual tours of other
kinds of schools.

A VIDEO TOUR
READING RAINBOW. Check your media
center or classroom library
for a video featuring a segment
from Reading Rainbow.

Review and Test Preparation

Visual Summary

Finish the table to show how schools are alike
and different.

Schools	
Alike	**Different**
Schools have teachers.	Schools are different sizes.
Everyone uses tools to learn.	Some classrooms have computers.

THINK & WRITE

Make a Choice Choose
a tool you use every day
in school.

Write a Label Write the
name of the tool. Tell how
it is used.

Use Vocabulary

Write the word that goes with each meaning.

1 a number of people working together

2 the leader of a school

3 an instruction telling what must be done

4 a person who helps others learn

5 to find out something new

> **learn**
> (p. 6)
> **rule**
> (p. 10)
> **group**
> (p. 12)
> **teacher**
> (p. 14)
> **principal**
> (p. 14)

Recall Facts

6 Name a school rule that helps children be fair.

7 What tools help you learn?

8 Tell two ways schools today are different from schools long ago.

9 Which of these school workers helps you find a book?

A nurse   **C** custodian

B librarian   **D** food server

10 Which of these is a good symbol for a cafeteria?

F   **H**

G   **J**

Think Critically

11 What can happen when people do not follow rules?

12 How is working in a group different from working alone?

Apply Chart and Graph Skills

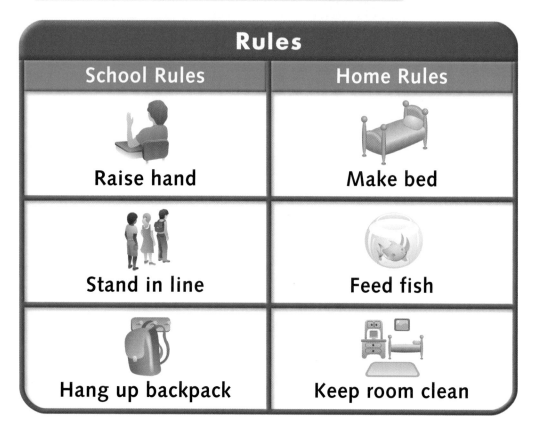

Rules	
School Rules	**Home Rules**
Raise hand	Make bed
Stand in line	Feed fish
Hang up backpack	Keep room clean

13 What is the title of this table?

14 Which side shows rules at school? Which side shows rules at home?

15 Is **Feed fish** a school or home rule?

16 On which side would the rule **Take turns** go?

38

Study these symbols.

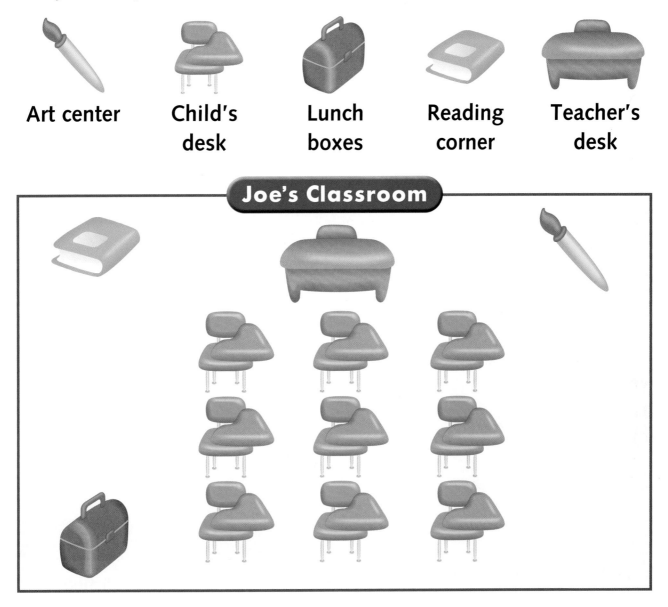

Art center   Child's desk   Lunch boxes   Reading corner   Teacher's desk

Joe's Classroom

⑰ What does this map show?

⑱ What is the symbol for the reading corner?

⑲ What is the brush a symbol for?

⑳ What is between the art center and the reading corner?

Unit Activities

Complete the Unit Project   Work with your group to finish the unit project. Decide what you want to show in your scrapbook. Make a cover.

GO ONLINE

Visit The Learning Site at **www.harcourtschool.com/ socialstudies/activities** for additional activities.

Sunrise Elementary Open House Night

Come meet the teacher and see how we are learning!

Wednesday, September 10th 7:00 p.m.

Mr. Stevens

Book

Our class pet, Whiskers

Choose a Place

Choose one of these places in your school. Draw a picture of it.
- classroom
- cafeteria
- library

Match Workers and Tools

Draw pictures of school workers. Find or draw pictures of the tools they use at work. Match the workers to their tools.

Visit Your Library

Get Up and Go! by Stuart J. Murphy. Follow a young girl as she gets ready for school on a busy morning.

First Day, Hooray! by Nancy Poydar. Workers and students are getting  ready for the first day of school.

A School Album by Peter and Connie Roop. See how schools long ago and today are alike and different.

Good Citizens

An airplane hood ornament
for car, 1915

Good Citizens

" I pledge allegiance to my flag. "

—Francis Bellamy, in the magazine *Youth's Companion*, September 8, 1892

Preview the Content

Make a chart to show what you know and what you want to know about being a good citizen. At the end of this unit, finish the chart with what you learned.

K-W-L Chart		
What I Know	What I Want to Know	What I Learned

law A rule that people in a community must follow. (page 46)

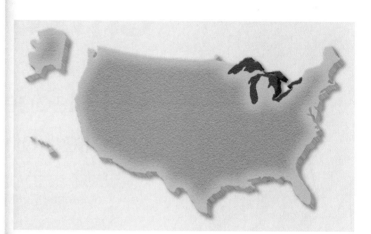

country An area of land with its own people and laws. (page 52)

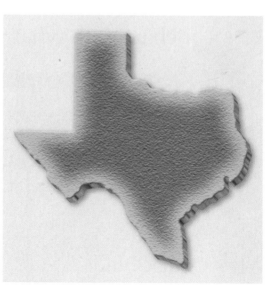

state A part of a country. (page 52)

42

President The leader of the United States government. (page 54)

flag A piece of cloth with a special design that stands for a country or group. (page 62)

citizen A person who lives in and belongs to a community. (page 68)

43

America

by Samuel F. Smith
illustrated by Erika LeBarre

My country, 'tis of thee,
Sweet land of liberty,
Of thee I sing.
Land where my fathers died,
Land of the Pilgrims' pride,
From every mountainside
Let freedom ring!

My native country, thee,
Land of the noble free,
Thy name I love.
I love thy rocks and rills,
Thy woods and templed hills;
My heart with rapture thrills
Like that above.

Read a Book

Visit the Capitol

Philadelphia Home of Liberty

at the Eiffel Tower

Think About It

1. What does the author tell us about America?

2. How does the song make you feel?

Start the Unit Project

Proud Citizens Mobile Your class will make a mobile that shows people being proud citizens. As you read this unit, think about how we show pride in our community, state, and country.

Use Technology

Visit The Learning Site at **www.harcourtschool.com/ socialstudies** for additional activities, primary sources, and other resources to use in this unit.

45

Rules and Laws

A community has rules called laws. A **law** is a rule that people in a community must follow. A **community** is a group of people who live or work together. It is also the place where those people live.

Police officers work to keep people safe.
They make sure that people obey the laws.

LESSON 1
Review

❶ **Vocabulary** Explain why **communities** need **laws**.

❷ How are rules and laws the same? How are they different?

❸ Make a sign for a law in your community that helps keep people safe.

Who Are Our Leaders?

Main Idea
Leaders help people follow rules and laws.

Vocabulary

leader

mayor

city

governor

government

You belong to many groups. You are a member of a family, a class, and a school. Most groups have leaders. A **leader** is in charge of helping a group of people follow rules.

Communities also have leaders. A **mayor** is the leader of a city or town. A **city** is a large, busy community. A mayor works with other leaders to make a community a good place to live.

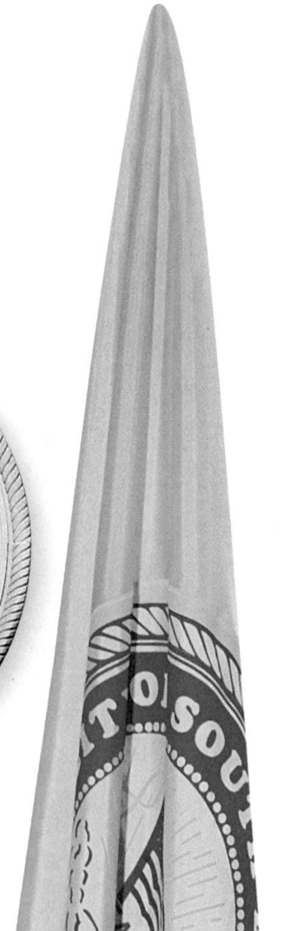

Mayor
Stephen Luecke
of South Bend,
Indiana

50

A **governor** is also a leader. The governor works for many communities.

Mayors and governors are part of the government. The **government** is a group of people who make laws. Government workers also do other jobs in a community, such as repairing roads, keeping parks in good condition, and helping when there is a fire.

Work with your leaders.

LESSON 2 Review

1 **Vocabulary** What do **leaders** do?

2 How can you help leaders at school and in the community?

3 Pretend you are the leader of a group. Tell how you would help the group members.

Find States on a Map

Vocabulary

country

state

border

▶ Why It Matters

A **country** is an area of land with its own people and laws. Our country is the United States of America. The United States is made up of 50 states. A **state** is one part of our country.

▶ What You Need to Know

On a map, lines called borders separate states and countries. A **border** shows where a state or country ends. The countries of Canada and Mexico have borders that touch the United States.

Welcome to Virginia

United States

Practice the Skill

1 Which state shares a border with Maine?

2 Locate your state. Name a state that is near yours.

3 How many states share Virginia's border?

Apply What You Learned

List the states with borders that touch Canada or Mexico.

Practice your map and globe skills with the **GeoSkills CD-ROM.**

Main Idea
The President is the leader of our country.

Vocabulary
President

Our Country's Presidents

The **President** is the leader of our country. The President and other government leaders work together to decide on laws.

Much of the President's work is done at the White House. The White House is also the home of the President.

The President meets with people and leaders from around our country. The President visits leaders in other countries, too.

The White House

George Washington was the first President of the United States of America. He did not live in the White House, but he helped decide where to build it.

George Washington was the first person to sign the Constitution of the United States. The Constitution is the plan for our country's government. Our country still follows this plan today.

The Constitution of the United States of America

Thomas Jefferson
1743–1826
Character Trait: Responsibility

Thomas Jefferson was the third President of our country. In 1776 he helped write the Declaration of Independence, which started the United States.

MULTIMEDIA BIOGRAPHIES
Visit The Learning Site at
www.harcourtschool.com/biographies
to learn about other famous people.

The Constitution says that Americans can choose who will be President. Our country has had 43 Presidents.

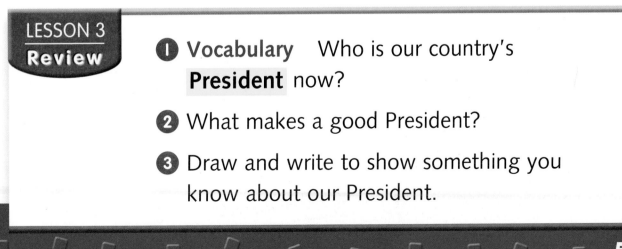

LESSON 3
Review

❶ **Vocabulary** Who is our country's **President** now?

❷ What makes a good President?

❸ Draw and write to show something you know about our President.

Make a Choice by Voting

Vocabulary

vote

ballot

▶ Why It Matters

Americans vote for many government leaders. When you **vote**, you make a choice. Americans also vote to make choices about laws.

▶ What You Need to Know

Americans use a **ballot** to vote. A ballot is a paper that shows all of the choices. You mark on it what your choice is. When voting time is over, the votes for each choice are counted. The choice with the most votes wins.

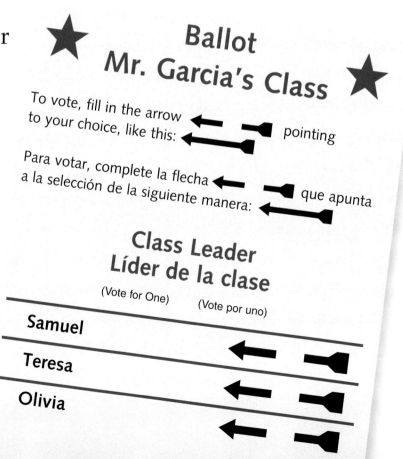

★ **Ballot** ★
Mr. Garcia's Class

To vote, fill in the arrow pointing
to your choice, like this:

Para votar, complete la flecha
a la selección de la siguiente manera: que apunta

Class Leader
Líder de la clase

(Vote for One)   (Vote por uno)

Samuel

Teresa

Olivia

58

▶ Practice the Skill

1 Mr. Garcia's class used ballots to vote for a class leader. The choices were Samuel, Teresa, and Olivia. The votes were counted. Look at the chart to see who got the most votes.

2 Who will be the class leader?

▶ Apply What You Learned

Have a class vote. Make a list of books your class would like to read. Make a ballot showing all of the choices. Count the votes each book gets. Show the counts on a chart. Which book does your class most want to read?

America's Symbols

Main Idea
Symbols remind us to show respect for our country.

Vocabulary
flag

The United States of America has symbols that remind us of important people and events. Some of these symbols are places we can visit.

Bald eagle

Capitol building

FAST FACT A leader named Benjamin Franklin wanted the turkey to be a symbol of the United States. The bald eagle was chosen instead.

Mount Rushmore

The Alamo

Washington Monument

Liberty Bell

Statue of Liberty

61

Our **flag** is a symbol of our country. It is red, white, and blue. Each star stands for one of the states in our country. The stripes stand for the first 13 states in the United States. When we say the Pledge of Allegiance, we show that our country is important to us.

The Pledge of Allegiance

I pledge allegiance to the Flag
of the United States of America,
and to the Republic
for which it stands,
one Nation under God, indivisible,
with liberty and justice for all.

Each state has its own flag.

Some states have pledges to their flags.

Honor the Texas flag.
I pledge allegiance to thee,
Texas, one and indivisible.

I Salute
the Arkansas Flag
With Its Diamond and Stars.
We Pledge
Our Loyalty to Thee.

Our country has the motto, or saying, "In God We Trust." States have mottoes, too.

Pennsylvania

Virtue, Liberty, and Independence

Texas

Friendship

Indiana

The Crossroads of America

· HERITAGE ·

Washington State

The state of Washington was named for George Washington, the first President of the United States. It is the only state named for a President.

THE SEAL OF THE STATE OF WASHINGTON 1889

We can sing songs that show how proud we
are of our country and our state.

1 **Vocabulary**   Explain how the **flag** is a symbol for our country.

2 Do you think symbols are important? Why?

3 Make a poster to show symbols of your state.

Fiction or Nonfiction

Vocabulary

fiction

nonfiction

fact

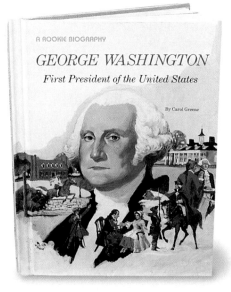

▶ **Why It Matters**

Stories can be made up or real. Made-up stories are **fiction**. Books of real information are **nonfiction**. Nonfiction books tell only facts. A **fact** is something that is true.

▶ **What You Need to Know**

The title, pictures, and words of a book let you know if it's fiction or nonfiction.

Then, in 1789, George was elected the first president of the United States.

He didn't think he was good enough to be president. But he took the job.

Practice the Skill

1 Look at the two books.

2 Which book do you think is fiction? What makes you think so?

3 Which book do you think tells more facts? What makes you think so?

Apply What You Learned

Choose a book, and look at the cover and the pictures. Do you think the book is fiction or nonfiction? How can you tell?

5

Portraits of Good Citizens

Main Idea
Good citizens help others.

Vocabulary

citizen

A **citizen** is a person who lives in and belongs to a community. Good citizens do things to help people. Read about the ways these good citizens helped others.

Patriotism

Nathan Hale
1755–1776
Character Trait: Patriotism

Nathan Hale showed great patriotism, or love for his country. He was a leader who helped Americans fight to be free from the country of England.

Responsibility

Sam Houston
1793–1863
Character Trait: Responsibility

When Sam Houston moved to Texas, it belonged to Mexico. He helped when the Americans living there fought to be free from Mexico. He also worked to make Texas part of the United States.

Compassion

Clara Barton
1821–1912
Character Trait: Compassion

Clara Barton started the American Red Cross. The Red Cross is a group that helps when something bad happens, such as a flood. It gives people food, clothing, and a place to stay.

Fairness

Eleanor Roosevelt
1884–1962
Character Trait: Fairness

Eleanor Roosevelt believed that everyone should be treated fairly. She worked with leaders of other countries to help people all over the world have better lives.

Inventiveness

Stephanie Kwolek
born in 1923
Character Trait: Inventiveness

Stephanie Kwolek made an important new fabric. This material is light but stronger than steel. It is used in the special vests police officers wear. Her discovery has helped save many lives.

Civic Virtue

Firefighters
Character Trait: Civic Virtue

Some citizens have dangerous jobs. When firefighters are called to work, they do all they can to help people. They will even give up their own safety.

Many firefighters lost their lives when buildings in New York City were attacked on September 11, 2001.

❶ **Vocabulary** What are some ways people can be good **citizens**?

❷ What are some character traits of good citizens?

❸ Think about a good citizen you know. Tell the class about him or her.

Rights and Responsibilities

Main Idea
Citizens have rights and responsibilities.

Vocabulary

right
responsibility

Citizens of our country have special rights. A **right** is something people are free to do. They can choose their leaders. They can belong to groups. They can live where they want to live.

Freedom of religion

Freedom of speech

When people have rights, they also have responsibilities. A **responsibility** is something you should take care of or do. One responsibility is to obey laws. This keeps the community safe.

IT'S THE LAW
clean up after your dog
maximum fine $100
public health law 1310
DEPARTMENT OF SANITATION

LESSON 6
Review

❶ **Vocabulary** What is one **right** that Americans have?

❷ What responsibilities do you have at school?

❸ Draw a picture that shows a responsibility you have at home.

How Communities Honor Their Citizens

Get Ready

Many communities celebrate people who have done something special. They may name a street, park, or building for such a person.

What to See

This school is named for the poet Gwendolyn Brooks. She wrote poems about people in her neighborhood.

This mural is about the work of architect Daniel Burnham. He planned parks and buildings that gave cities a special look.

PASTEUR PARK
CHICAGO PARK DISTRICT

Pasteur Park is named for a scientist. Louis Pasteur found a way to kill germs in food we eat.

Take a Field Trip

GO ONLINE

A VIRTUAL TOUR
Visit The Learning Site at www.harcourtschool.com/tours to take virtual tours of other monuments and memorials.

READING RAINBOW.

A VIDEO TOUR
Check your media center or classroom library for a video featuring a segment from Reading Rainbow.

Unit 2

Review and Test Preparation

Visual Summary

Finish the chart to show what you have learned about being a good citizen.

K-W-L Chart

What I Know	What I Want to Know	What I Learned
We have laws.	Does everyone have to follow laws?	
We have a President.	Who is our President?	

THINK & WRITE

Talk About It   Think about some of the symbols of our country. Talk about what the symbols mean.

Write a Sentence   Choose a symbol. Write a sentence telling why it is a good symbol for our country.

Write the word that goes with each picture.

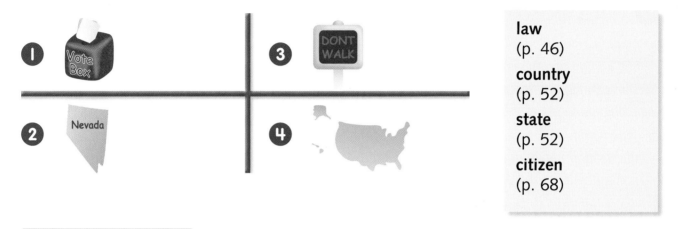

1

2 Nevada

3 DONT WALK

4

law
(p. 46)

country
(p. 52)

state
(p. 52)

citizen
(p. 68)

Recall Facts

5 What is a law?

6 Name leaders in your community and state.

7 How are a country and a state different?

8 Who was the first President of the United States?

9 Which of these is the home of the President of the United States?

    A Capitol building   **C** Alamo

    B Washington Monument   **D** White House

10 Which of these tells about nonfiction books?

    F tell no facts   **H** have real information

    G have no pictures   **J** have made-up stories

11 How do leaders help citizens?

12 What are some things that good citizens do?

Apply Chart and Graph Skills

Class Field Trip Votes	
museum	| | | |
zoo	| | | | | | | | | | |
park	| | | | | | | |

13 What are the children in Mrs. Johnson's class voting about?

14 What are the choices?

15 How many votes does the museum have?

16 Which choice has the most votes?

United States

17 Find Indiana. Name the states that share borders with Indiana.

18 What countries share borders with the United States?

19 Which state is closer to Canada, Montana or North Carolina?

20 Which state shares a border with Nebraska, Iowa or Texas?

Unit Activities

GO ONLINE

Visit The Learning Site at **www.harcourtschool.com/ socialstudies/activities** for additional activities.

Complete the Unit Project Work with your group to finish the unit project. Decide how you will show what good citizens do and what is special about our country.

Choose a Leader

Draw one of these leaders. Write a sentence telling why he or she is a good leader. Add your leader to the mobile.

- teacher
- principal
- coach

American Symbols

Draw or find pictures of American symbols. You can also use your state's symbols. Add the symbols to the mobile.

Visit Your Library

The Inside-Outside Book of Washington, D.C. by Roxie Munro. Take a look at some of the important buildings in Washington, D.C.

If I Were President by Catherine Stier. Read about what some children would do if they were President of the United States.

The Flag We Love by Pam Muñoz Ryan. Find out facts about the flag of the United States.

The Land Around Us

The Land Around Us

> 66 Enjoy the earth gently
> Enjoy the earth gently
> For if the earth is spoiled
> It cannot be repaired
> Enjoy the earth gently. 99
>
> —Yoruba (African) song

Preview the Content

Make a web to show some of our world's natural resources. As you read this unit, add to the web. Write what you learn about Earth's land, water, and other resources.

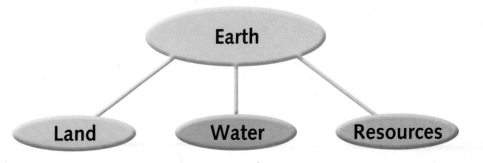

neighborhood The part of a community in which a group of people lives. (page 94)

continent One of seven main land areas on Earth. (page 105)

ocean A very large body of salty water. (page 105)

weather What the air outside is like. (page 112)

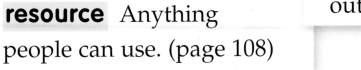

resource Anything people can use. (page 108)

From Here to There

by Margery Cuyler

illustrated by Yu Cha Pak

People often use their **address** to tell where they live. In this book, Maria describes where she lives in a special way.

My name is Maria Mendoza. I live with my
father, my mother, my baby brother, Tony,
and my older sister, Angelica,

at number 43 Juniper Street—

in the town of Splendora,

in the county of Montgomery,

in the state of Texas,

in the country of the United States,

89

on the continent of North America,

in the Western Hemisphere,

on the planet Earth,
in the solar system,

in the Milky Way galaxy,
in the universe
and beyond.

From here to there,
my name is
Maria Mendoza.

Think About It

1. How does Maria describe where she lives?

2. Write your address on an envelope.

Read a Book

Start the Unit Project

A Community Collage Your class will make a collage to show the kinds of land, water, and resources in and around your community. As you read this unit, remember how these things are important.

Use Technology

 Visit The Learning Site at **www.harcourtschool.com/ socialstudies** for additional activities, primary sources, and other resources to use in this unit.

A Neighborhood

Main Idea
People in a neighborhood share things.

Vocabulary

neighborhood

Not far from Splendora, where Maria lives, is the city of Houston. Houston is a large community with many neighborhoods. A **neighborhood** is a small part of a community in which people live. People in a neighborhood share schools, libraries, parks, and other places of the community.

Look at this picture of a Houston neighborhood taken from above.

This is a map of the same neighborhood.

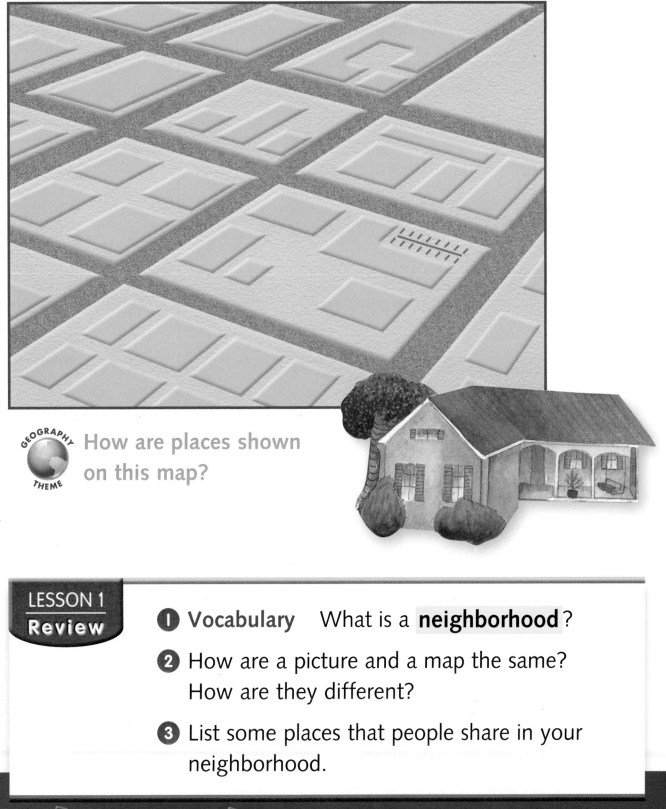

GEOGRAPHY THEME

How are places shown
on this map?

LESSON 1
Review

1 **Vocabulary**   What is a **neighborhood**?

2 How are a picture and a map the same?
How are they different?

3 List some places that people share in your
neighborhood.

Use a Map Key

Vocabulary

map key

▶ **Why It Matters**

Symbols help you find places on a map.

▶ **What You Need to Know**

A **map key** lists the symbols used on a map. It shows you what they mean.

▶ **Practice the Skill**

❶ What is the symbol for the zoo?

❷ Find the Community Center. On what street is it located?

❸ What is near the lake?

Map Key

🏠	Children's Museum
🏢	Community Center
⛳	Golf Course
🏛	Houston Museum of Natural Science
🏯	Japanese Garden
🏫	Rice University
🐅	Zoo
☐	Street

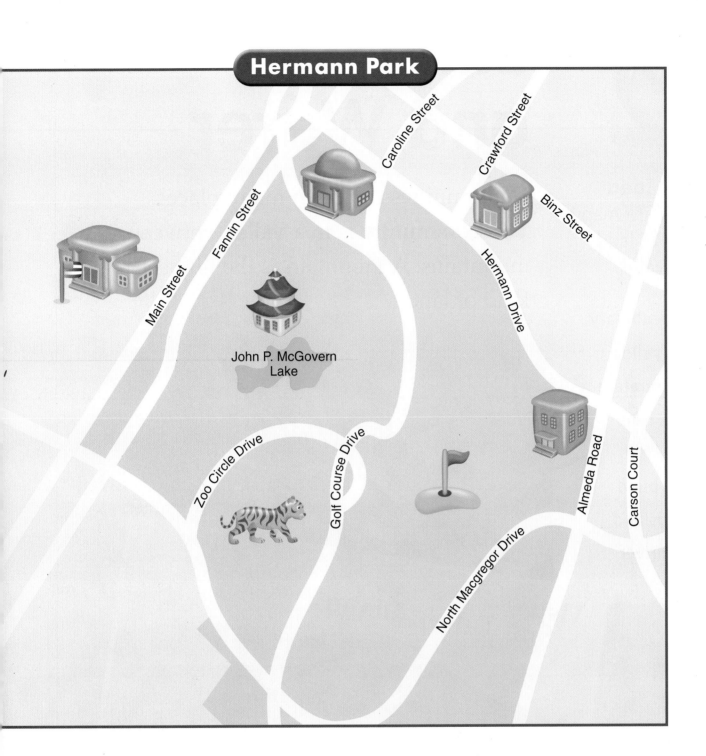

Hermann Park

- Caroline Street
- Crawford Street
- Fannin Street
- Binz Street
- Main Street
- Hermann Drive
- John P. McGovern Lake
- Zoo Circle Drive
- Golf Course Drive
- Almeda Road
- Carson Court
- North Macgregor Drive

▶ Apply What You Learned

Make a map of your community.

Use symbols and a map key.

 Practice your map and globe skills with the **GeoSkills CD-ROM.**

Land and Water

Main Idea
There are many kinds of land and water.

Communities can be in many places. This community is in a **valley** between mountains. A **mountain** is the highest kind of land.

Vocabulary

valley

mountain

lake

hill

plain

island

river

Sawtooth Mountains

Dear Aunt Patty,

I'm having a great time in Sun Valley!

Love,
Tony

Visit Sun Valley, Idaho

This community is near a lake. There is land all around the water of a **lake**. Lakes can be large or small, shallow or deep.

Sun Valley
Aug '04, 2003
Idaho, USA

California
USA

California Quail & California Poppy

Patty Hosley
1234 Sea Dr.
Orlando, FL 12345

Silver Lake,
Massachusetts

There are other kinds of land. A **hill** is land that rises above the land around it. Hills are not as high as mountains.

The Hills of California

A **plain** is land that is mostly flat. The land in most plains is good for growing food.

Main Street
Lawrence, Kansas

Across Kansas
Plains

An **island** is land that has water all around it.

NORWALK ISLANDS

Connecticut, U.S.A.

Love, Patty

575 Penn Lane
York, PA 17404

NORWALK, CT
PM
04 AUG
2003

COLORADO RIVER

ARIZONA, USA

A **river** is a long body of moving water that moves across the land. The water in some rivers flows very fast.

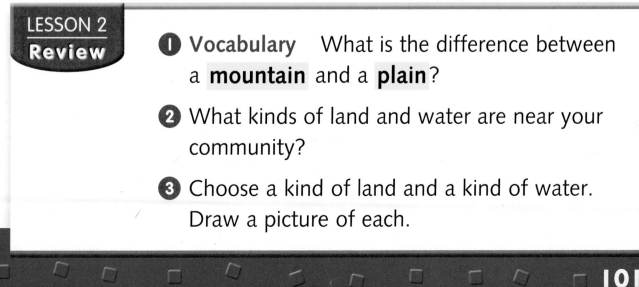

LESSON 2 Review

❶ **Vocabulary** What is the difference between a **mountain** and a **plain**?

❷ What kinds of land and water are near your community?

❸ Choose a kind of land and a kind of water. Draw a picture of each.

Find Land and Water on a Map

▶ Why It Matters

Seeing land and water on maps can help you imagine what places look like.

▶ What You Need to Know

Texas is a large state. It has many kinds of land and water. Different colors show the different kinds of land and water.

▶ Practice the Skill

1 Describe the symbols for land and water on the map.

2 Name two rivers in Texas.

3 Which city is found in the mountains?

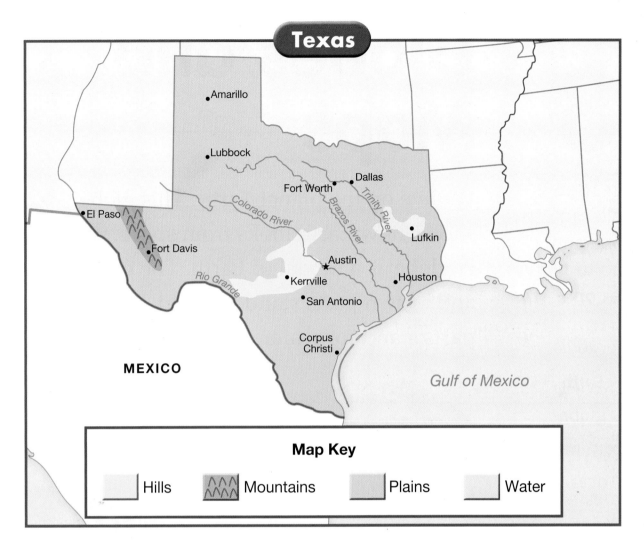

Texas

Amarillo

Lubbock

Fort Worth • Dallas

El Paso

Colorado River

Brazos River

Trinity River

Lufkin

Fort Davis

Rio Grande

Austin

Kerrville

San Antonio

Houston

Corpus
Christi

MEXICO

Gulf of Mexico

Map Key

Hills   Mountains   Plains   Water

▶ Apply What You Learned

Look at a map of your state. Find the
different kinds of land and water.

MAP AND GLOBE
SKILLS

Practice your map and globe skills
with the **GeoSkills CD-ROM.**

3

Globes and Maps

Main Idea

People can use a globe and a map to find places on Earth.

Vocabulary

Earth

globe

continent

ocean

We live on the planet **Earth**. This globe shows how Earth looks from space. A **globe** is a model of Earth. The green and brown parts stand for land. The blue parts stand for water.

Like a globe, a map can also show all the places on Earth. The seven large areas of land are **continents**. We live on the continent of North America. Between most of the continents are oceans. An **ocean** is a very large body of salty water.

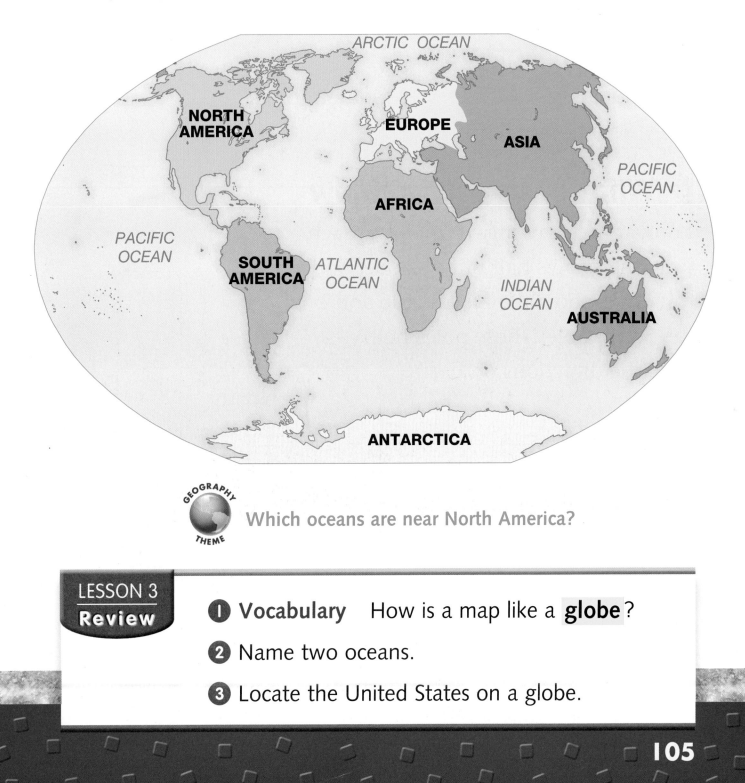

GEOGRAPHY THEME

Which oceans are near North America?

LESSON 3 Review

1 **Vocabulary** How is a map like a **globe**?

2 Name two oceans.

3 Locate the United States on a globe.

Find Directions on a Globe

Vocabulary

directions

▶ Why It Matters

Directions show or tell where something is. They help you find a place.

▶ What You Need to Know

Look at the drawings of a globe. Each drawing shows half of the globe. Both drawings show the North Pole and the South Pole. These poles help describe directions on Earth.

The main directions are north, south, east, and west. North is the direction toward the North Pole. When you face north, east is to your right. West is to your left.

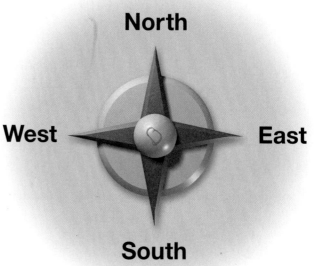

North

West   East

South

▶ Practice the Skill

① Which continent is east of Europe?

② Which continent is at the South Pole?

③ Which ocean is west of North America?

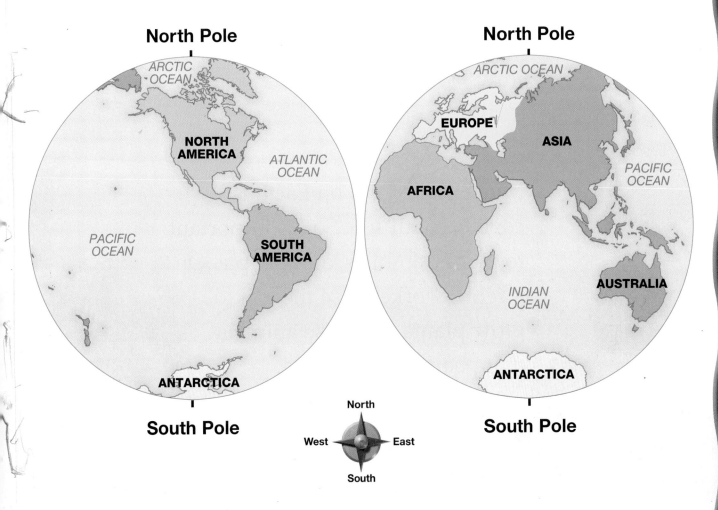

▶ Apply What You Learned

Make a model of Earth.

 Practice your map and globe skills with the **GeoSkills CD-ROM**.

People and Resources

Main Idea
Natural resources are important to people.

Vocabulary

resource

farm

forest

How are paper, bread, and gasoline alike? They are all made from Earth's resources. A **resource** is anything people can use. Earth has many resources.

Soil

Much of the land on Earth is covered with soil. Soil is important to plants, animals, and people. On a **farm**, workers use the soil to grow plants and raise animals that people use for food.

108

Trees

A **forest** is a large area where many trees grow. Wood from trees is used to make furniture and buildings. Some trees give us food, such as apples and walnuts.

Oil and Gas

Oil and gas come from under the ground. People use oil and gas to heat their homes and cook their food. Some oil is made into gasoline for running cars and other machines.

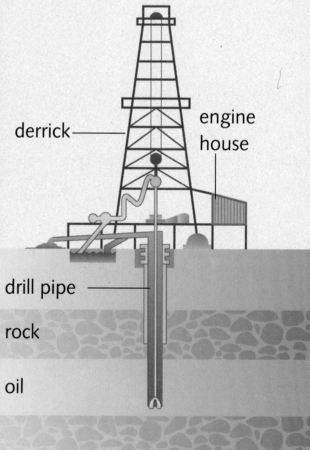

A CLOSER LOOK
Drilling for Oil

People drill holes deep into the ground to reach oil. An engine turns the drill pipe so that it cuts down through rock in the ground. When the drill reaches oil, the oil is pumped up through the pipe. **How do people reach the oil under the ground?**

derrick

engine house

drill pipe

rock

oil

Water

Water is a resource that all living things must have to live. People and animals drink it, and some plants and animals live in it.

LESSON 4
Review

① **Vocabulary** How do **resources** help you?

② What natural resources are in or near your community?

③ Make a list of ways people use water.

Predict What Will Happen

Vocabulary

predict

weather

▶ Why It Matters

When you know how things happen, you can **predict**, or tell ahead of time, what will happen next. Knowing what is going to happen can help people plan what to do.

▶ What You Need to Know

People can predict the weather by looking at clouds. **Weather** is what the air outside is like. Dark clouds often mean rain is coming.

Practice the Skill

1. If it did not rain for a long time, what would happen to growing food?

2. Think about the people who make, sell, and buy food. Tell what you think would happen to them.

Apply What You Learned

What do you think would happen if people caught all the fish they could find?

113

Saving Our Resources

Main Idea
People need to take care of Earth's natural resources.

Vocabulary

pollution

litter

recycle

Many people live on Earth. They all use the same resources.

Protect Our Resources

It is important to keep earth and our resources clean. **Pollution** is anything that makes air, land, or water dirty.

Laws help. You can help, too. Do not **litter**, or throw trash, on land or in water.

Marjory Stoneman Douglas
1890–1998
Character Trait: Responsibility

Marjory Stoneman Douglas loved the Everglades, the low, wet grasslands in southern Florida. Thanks to her help, laws now protect the Everglades and its wildlife.

MULTIMEDIA BIOGRAPHIES
Visit The Learning Site at
www.harcourtschool.com/biographies
to learn about other famous people.

GO ONLINE

Use Resources Wisely

You can reduce, or use less of a resource.

You can reuse, or use some things over and over again.

116

Reduce, reuse, recycle.

You can **recycle**, or make something old into something new.

Recycle

LESSON 5
Review

❶ **Vocabulary** Why is it important not to **litter**?

❷ Why should people use less of a resource?

❸ Make a poster showing how you can use resources wisely at home.

6

Main Idea
People around the world live in all kinds of homes.

Vocabulary

desert

Houses and Homes

People around the world have different kinds of homes. Some live in houses. Others live in buildings with many apartments.

Germany

Canada

Brazil

People build homes using the resources of the land where they live. These homes in Congo have roofs made from straw, or dried grass.

Congo

Mexico

People also have to think about the weather where they build their homes. This place in Mexico is built of clay bricks dried in the hot desert sun. A **desert** is land that gets little rain.

.GEOGRAPHY.

GEOGRAPHY ESSENTIAL ELEMENTS

The saguaro cactus grows in the Sonoran Desert. This desert is in the southern part of the United States and the northern part of Mexico.

UNITED STATES

MEXICO

Sonoran Desert

This house is in Norway. It is made from the trees in the forest around it.

Norway

When it rains a lot, this river in the Amazon rain forest can flood. This house in Venezuela is built on stilts. They keep it dry above the river's water.

Venezuela

Some places are crowded. These homes in Italy are built close together. There is little open space between the homes.

Italy

China

This city in China has very little land for new homes. Some people live on boats.

LESSON 6
Review

1 **Vocabulary**   How is a **desert** different from a forest?

2 Why do people have to think about the weather when they build their homes?

3 Describe the types of houses in your neighborhood.

A Butterfly Garden

Get Ready

Planting a flower garden makes any place more beautiful. Some flowers are favorites of butterflies. These students decided to plant a butterfly garden outside their school.

What to See

Each student draws a plan for the new butterfly garden.

Then

Butterfly gardens need to get lots of sun but not much wind.

The students work in the garden to care for the flowers.

Now

Students celebrate the new garden with a party.

Take a Field Trip

GO ONLINE

A VIRTUAL TOUR
Visit The Learning Site at **www.harcourtschool.com/tours** to take virtual tours of other parks and scenic areas.

A VIDEO TOUR
Check your media center or classroom library for a video featuring a segment from Reading Rainbow.

Review and Test Preparation

Complete this web. Write or draw to show what you learned in this unit.

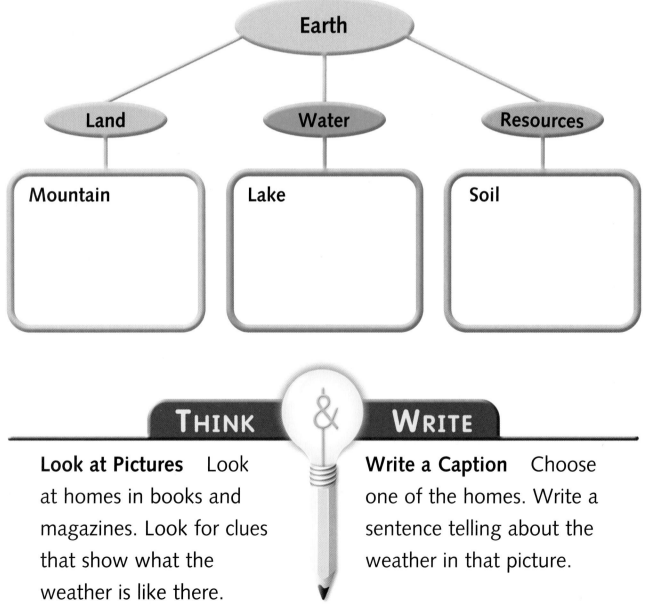

Earth

Land

Water

Resources

Mountain

Lake

Soil

THINK & WRITE

Look at Pictures Look at homes in books and magazines. Look for clues that show what the weather is like there.

Write a Caption Choose one of the homes. Write a sentence telling about the weather in that picture.

Use Vocabulary

Draw a picture to show the meaning of each word.

1 neighborhood

(p. 94)

3 resource

(p. 108)

2 ocean

(p. 105)

4 weather

(p. 112)

Recall Facts

5 How many continents are there?

6 How are a river and an ocean different?

7 Name two kinds of resources.

8 How do farmers use soil?

9 On which continent do you live?

A Africa

C North America

B Australia

D South America

10 Which resource do people use to build homes?

F water

H oil

G soil

J trees

11 How can being able to predict what will happen help people plan what to do?

12 Why is it important to take care of Earth's resources?

Apply Map and Globe Skills

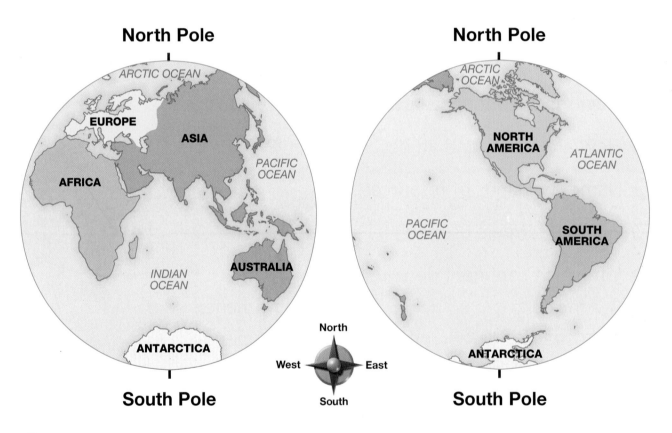

13 If you traveled south from North America, on what continent would you be?

14 Which ocean is west of Australia?

15 Is Antarctica north or south of Africa?

16 Which ocean is at the North Pole?

126

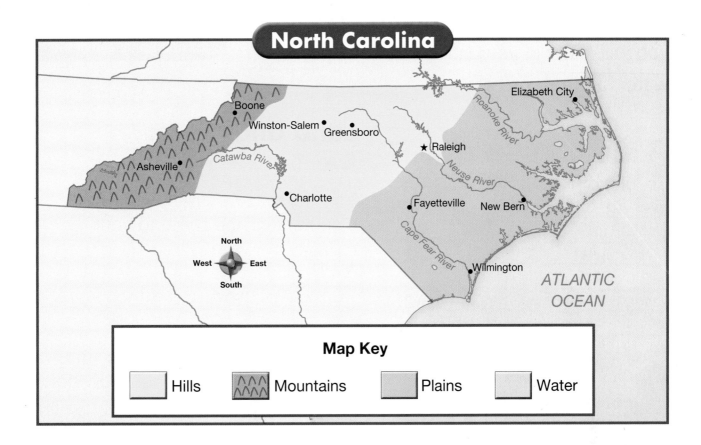

North Carolina

Map Key

Hills | Mountains | Plains | Water

17 Name the ocean that is east of North Carolina.

18 What kind of land is around Boone?

19 What kind of land is in the middle of the state?

20 Name a city that is on the plains.

Unit Activities

GO ONLINE

Visit The Learning Site at www.harcourtschool.com/socialstudies/activities for additional activities.

Complete the Unit Project Work with your group to finish the unit project. Decide what you will show in your collage about land, water, and resources.

Land and Water

Draw or find pictures that show the land and water around your community. Add these to your collage.

Using Resources

Draw or find pictures that show how people use these resources.
- soil
- trees
- oil and gas
- water

Visit Your Library

Compost! Growing Gardens from Your Garbage by Linda Glaser. Find out how a family recycles food leftovers.

Me on the Map by Joan Sweeney. A young girl shows where she is in the world.

Haystack by Bonnie and Arthur Geisert. See how important a haystack is on a farm.

All About People

Mexican maracas

All About People

❝We all sing with
the same voice.**❞**

—J. Phillip Miller, Sheppard McGreene, *Sesame Street*, 1983

Preview the Content

As you read, look for facts about culture. Write down the facts you find. After you read, write a sentence that tells the big idea of this unit.

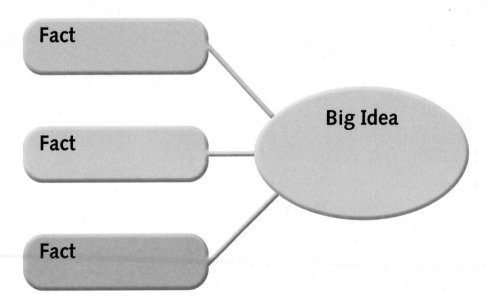

Fact

Fact

Big Idea

Fact

role The part a person plays in a group or community. (page 134)

needs Things people must have to live. (page 138)

culture A group's way of life. (page 143)

celebration A time to be happy about something special. (page 154)

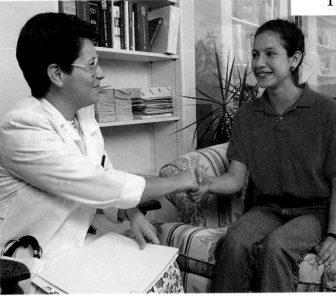

custom A group's way of doing something. (page 160)

The Mohawk Way

from *Time for Kids*

Kids at the Akwesasne (AH•kwe•zah•sneh) Freedom School in Rooseveltown, New York, don't speak English in class. They speak Mohawk, the **language** of their Native American ancestors. Children from kindergarten to sixth grade learn all their subjects in Mohawk. Learning about their own people makes the kids feel proud!

Kids enjoy Mohawk music and dancing.

132

Even art projects help kids learn about their tribe. This girl is building a paper longhouse.

A E I O En On
T K S R H N W

Ista means mom

How many?

The Mohawk language has 13 letters. English has 26 letters—twice as many.

Think About It

1 Why do the children at this school learn in a different language?

2 Find out about the Native Americans in your state.

Read a Book

Start the Unit Project

A World Culture Book Your class will make a book to show some of the cultures in our world. As you read this unit, think about how people are the same and different.

Use Technology

Visit The Learning Site at **www.harcourtschool.com/ socialstudies** for additional activities, primary sources, and other resources to use in this unit.

People Together

Main Idea
People have different roles in different groups.

Vocabulary

role

I belong to many groups. I am a member of my family, my class, my school, and more.

Each person in a group has a role. A **role** is the part that a person plays in a group he or she belongs to.

I am.

I am a daughter.
I set the table for dinner.

I am a first grader.
I water our class plants.

I am a soccer goalie.
I keep the other team
from scoring.

I am in an art club. I make
sure there are enough
brushes for everyone.

LESSON 1
Review

❶ **Vocabulary** What are your **roles** in school?

❷ How do you depend on other people in
your groups?

❸ Think about the groups you belong to. Make
a chart to show your role in each group.

Solve a Problem

Vocabulary

problem

solution

▶ Why It Matters

Sometimes people have problems. A **problem** is something that is hard to understand or to do. A problem needs a **solution**, or answer. You can work in a group to solve a problem.

▶ What You Need to Know

Follow these steps when you need to solve a problem.

Step 1 Name the problem.

Step 2 Think of some solutions.

Step 3 Talk about the solutions. Choose the best one.

Step 4 Follow your plan to solve the problem.

Step 5 Talk about how well the problem was solved.

▶ Practice the Skill

There are two computers in the classroom, and four children need to use them. Work in a group to solve this problem. Use the steps on page 136.

▶ Apply What You Learned

What would you do if you lost something you had borrowed? Write about how you would use the steps to solve the problem.

Families Together

Main Idea
People have needs that they meet in different ways.

All people have needs. **Needs** are things we must have to live. We must have food, clothing, and **shelter**, or a place to live in. Family members help take care of each other's needs.

food

clothing

shelter

139

food

Families all over the world have the same needs. Some meet their needs in the same ways your family does. Some meet their needs in different ways.

clothing

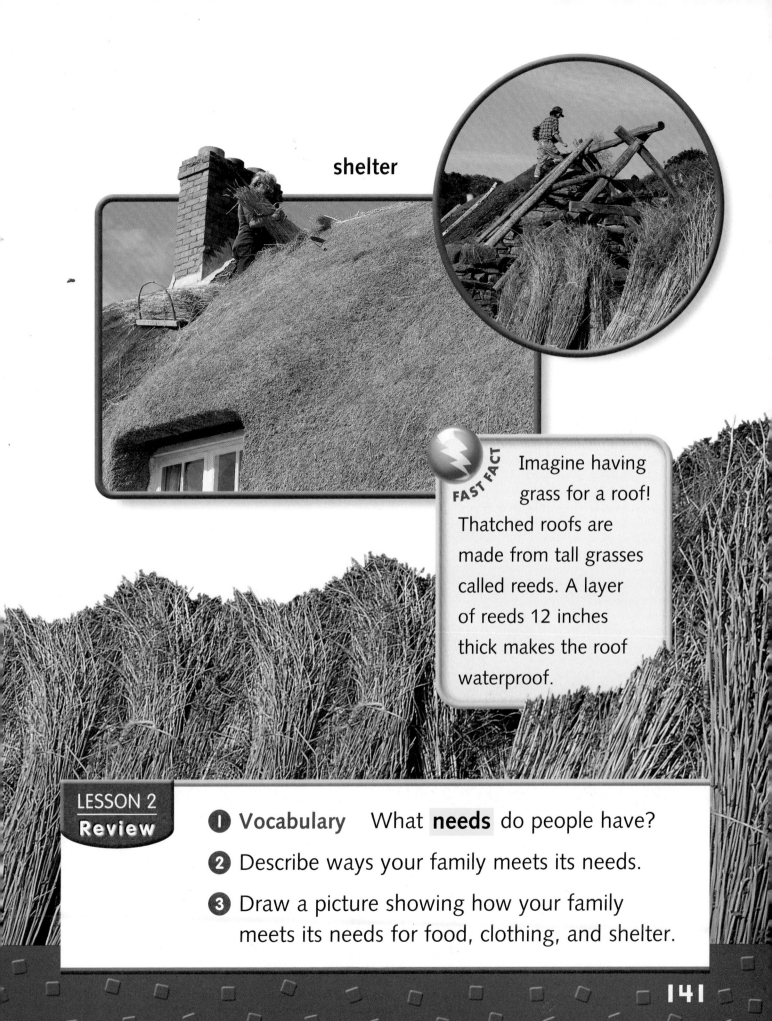

shelter

FAST FACT Imagine having grass for a roof! Thatched roofs are made from tall grasses called reeds. A layer of reeds 12 inches thick makes the roof waterproof.

LESSON 2
Review

1. **Vocabulary** What **needs** do people have?

2. Describe ways your family meets its needs.

3. Draw a picture showing how your family meets its needs for food, clothing, and shelter.

What Is Culture?

Main Idea
People around the world have different cultures.

My aunt Shelly loves to travel. She has met people who have different cultures.

They have great food in Denmark!

142

A **culture** is a group's way of life. I learned about cultures by helping my Aunt Shelly make this scrapbook.

Dolls from Peru

People sometimes wear kimonos in Japan.

This Inuit girl in Canada plays string games.

People in different culture groups
have different **religions**, or beliefs.

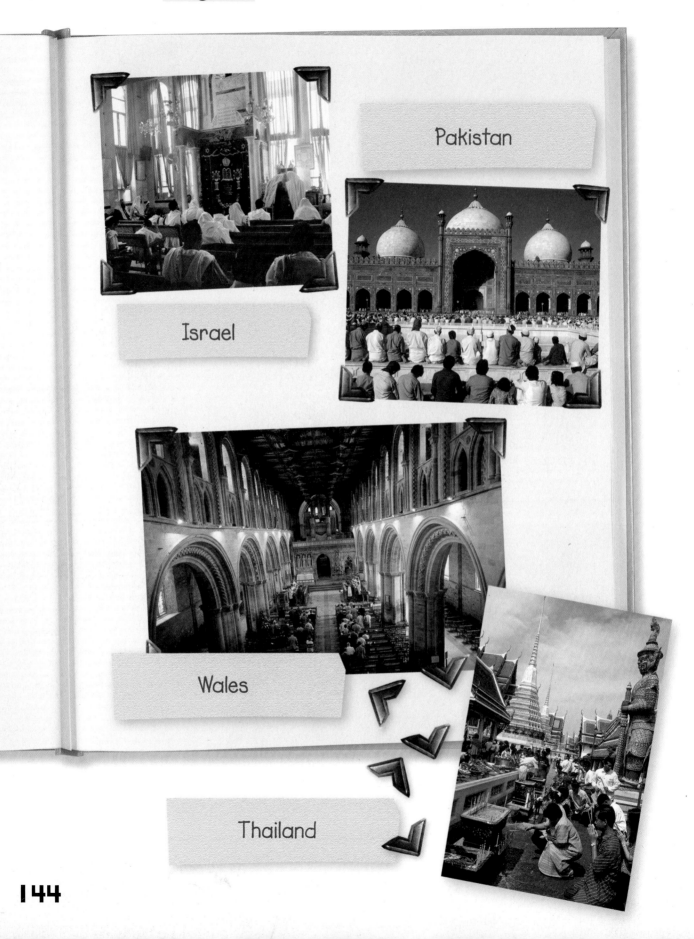

Pakistan

Israel

Wales

Thailand

Aunt Shelly learned how to say some things in different languages. <u>Friend</u> is one of her favorite words. <u>Tomodachi</u> means "friend" in Japanese.

TRAVEL LOG

LESSON 3
Review

❶ **Vocabulary**   What kinds of things are part of a group's **culture**?

❷ Why is language important?

❸ Cut out magazine pictures to make a poster about culture.

Point of View

Vocabulary

point of view

▶ Why It Matters

What is your favorite color? What is your friend's favorite color? You may think red is the best color. Your friend may think blue is. Not everyone thinks the same way. What you think is your **point of view**.

▶ What You Need to Know

Everyone needs to eat, but people like different kinds of food. Italian families eat many kinds of pasta. Chinese families eat a lot of rice. Different cultures have different points of view about foods.

146

▶ Practice the Skill

1 Look at the pictures of different breakfast foods. Which would you choose? Why?

2 Which is better, a hot breakfast or a cold breakfast? Why do you think so?

Scotland

China

Turkey

United States

▶ Apply What You Learned

Talk with your classmates about the foods you like best for lunch.

Expressing Culture

The foods people eat, the clothes they wear, and the languages they speak all show their culture. Music, dance, and other arts are also part of culture.

What do these pictures show about cultures?

Kente cloth from Ghana

Dancer from Thailand

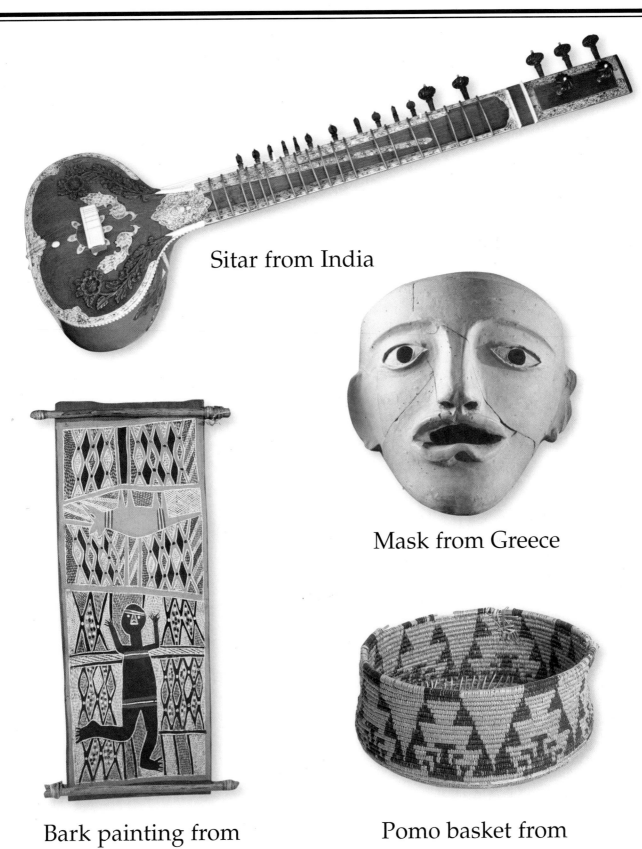

Sitar from India

Mask from Greece

Bark painting from
Australia

Pomo basket from
California

Stories are part of every culture. A **fable** is a made-up story that teaches a lesson. "The Hare and the Tortoise" is a fable that is still told today.

The Fables of Æsop

Selected, and their History traced, by Joseph Jacobs

Illustrated by Richard Heighway

1894 book

The Hare and the Tortoise

a fable by Aesop

Hare always boasted that he was the fastest animal. He made fun of Tortoise because she moved so slowly. One day Tortoise said, "If we raced, I might beat you. Let's race to the main road and see who wins."

Hare laughed, but he agreed to race. He started off at top speed and soon left Tortoise far behind. Hare was so sure he would win that he decided to take a nap.

Tortoise did not stop. She just kept going slow and steady. When Hare woke up, he saw that he had been wrong. Tortoise had won the race.

Lesson   The fastest one doesn't always get there first. Slow and steady wins the race.

Story cloth from Vietnam

Puppet from Indonesia

Activity

Make paper puppets of Tortoise and Hare.
Then use them to retell the story.

Research

GO ONLINE

Visit The Learning Site at
www.harcourtschool.com/primarysources
to research other primary sources.

Use a Map Scale

Vocabulary

distance

map scale

▶ Why It Matters

A map shows a place smaller than it really is, but it can show real distance. **Distance** is how far one place is from another.

▶ What You Need to Know

A map scale helps you find out how far apart places are. A **map scale**, like a ruler, is used to measure distance.

▶ Practice the Skill

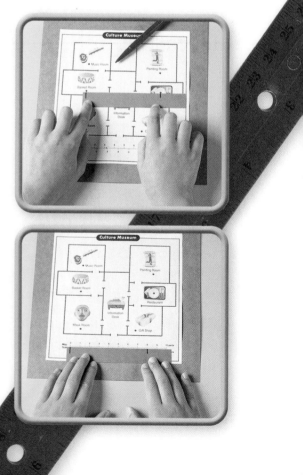

1 Lay a strip of paper so its edge touches the • in the Basket Room and the • in the Restaurant. Mark where each • is.

2 Place the paper along the map scale. One of the marks must be at zero.

3 How many yards are there between the two rooms?

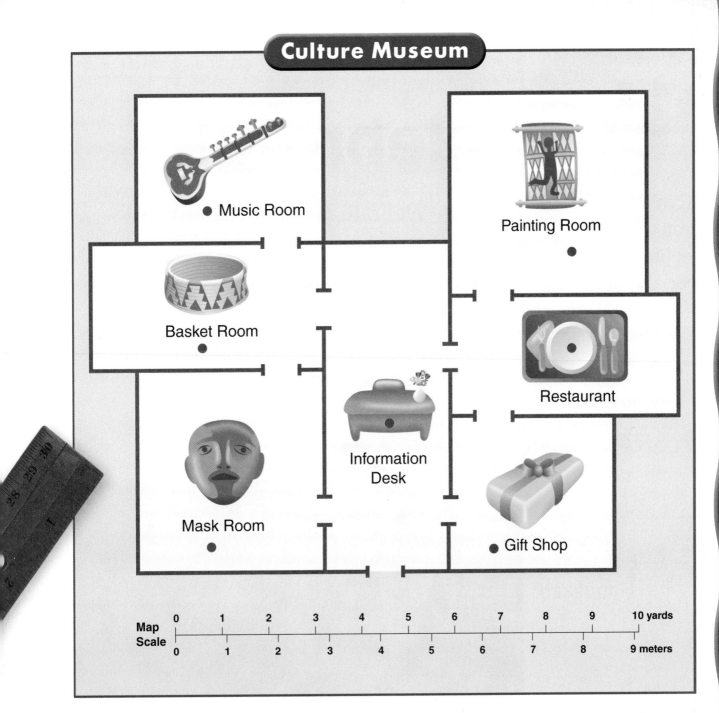

Culture Museum

Music Room

Painting Room

Basket Room

Restaurant

Mask Room

Information Desk

Gift Shop

Map Scale

| 0 | 1 | 2 | 3 | 4 | 5 | 6 | 7 | 8 | 9 | 10 yards |

| 0 | 1 | 2 | 3 | 4 | 5 | 6 | 7 | 8 | 9 meters |

▶ Apply What You Learned

Make a map of your classroom. Show a map scale and symbols.

MAP AND GLOBE SKILLS

Practice your map and globe skills with the **GeoSkills** CD-ROM.

Main Idea
People celebrate special times.

Vocabulary

celebration

holiday

Celebrate!

Families celebrate many special times. Some **celebrations**, such as birthday parties, are shared by only family and friends. Other celebrations, such as parades, are shared by many people on holidays. A **holiday** is a day for celebrating an event.

Hanukkah

On some holidays, people celebrate something in their religion. Families have special meals and activities on these days.

Christmas

Three Kings Day

Some celebrations come from other countries. When people move to the United States, they still celebrate the holidays they love. This helps them remember where they came from. Their celebrations show their culture.

Chinese New Year

Cinco de Mayo

Kwanzaa

Kwanzaa is a week-long holiday when African American families celebrate their culture. This holiday is new, but the ideas for it come from very old African beliefs. During Kwanzaa, families remember what is important to them.

Cherry Blossom Festival

Highland Games

All people are special.

LESSON 4
Review

1. **Vocabulary** How do **celebrations** teach us about other countries?

2. What are some things your family does to celebrate special times?

3. Make a greeting card for a holiday or a celebration.

Use a Calendar

Vocabulary

calendar

✳ 2003 ✳
December
22
Monday

▶ Why It Matters

A **calendar** is used to measure time.

▶ What You Need to Know

A calendar shows days, weeks, and months.
A week has 7 days. A year has 365 days in 52
weeks. There are also 12 months in a year.

January

S	M	T	W	Th	F	S
			1	2	3	4
5	6	7	8	9	10	11
12	13	14	15	16	17	18
19	20	21	22	23	24	25
26	27	28	29	30	31	

February

S	M	T	W	Th	F	S
						1
2	3	4	5	6	7	8
9	10	11	12	13	14	15
16	17	18	19	20	21	22
23	24	25	26	27	28	

March

S	M	T	W	Th	F	S
						1
2	3	4	5	6	7	8
9	10	11	12	13	14	15
16	17	18	19	20	21	22
23	24	25	26	27	28	29
30	31					

April

S	M	T	W	Th	F	S
		1	2	3	4	5
6	7	8	9	10	11	12
13	14	15	16	17	18	19
20	21	22	23	24	25	26
27	28	29	30			

May

S	M	T	W	Th	F	S
				1	2	3
4	5	6	7	8	9	10
11	12	13	14	15	16	17
18	19	20	21	22	23	24
25	26	27	28	29	30	31

June

S	M	T	W	Th	F	S
1	2	3	4	5	6	7
8	9	10	11	12	13	14
15	16	17	18	19	20	21
22	23	24	25	26	27	28
29	30					

July

S	M	T	W	Th	F	S
		1	2	3	4	5
6	7	8	9	10	11	12
13	14	15	16	17	18	19
20	21	22	23	24	25	26
27	28	29	30	31		

August

S	M	T	W	Th	F	S
					1	2
3	4	5	6	7	8	9
10	11	12	13	14	15	16
17	18	19	20	21	22	23
24	25	26	27	28	29	30
31						

September

S	M	T	W	Th	F	S
	1	2	3	4	5	6
7	8	9	10	11	12	13
14	15	16	17	18	19	20
21	22	23	24	25	26	27
28	29	30				

October

S	M	T	W	Th	F	S
			1	2	3	4
5	6	7	8	9	10	11
12	13	14	15	16	17	18
19	20	21	22	23	24	25
26	27	28	29	30	31	

November

S	M	T	W	Th	F	S
						1
2	3	4	5	6	7	8
9	10	11	12	13	14	15
16	17	18	19	20	21	22
23	24	25	26	27	28	29
30						

December

S	M	T	W	Th	F	S
	1	2	3	4	5	6
7	8	9	10	11	12	13
14	15	16	17	18	19	20
21	22	23	24	25	26	27
28	29	30	31			

▶ Practice the Skill

1 Look at the calendar. How many days are in December?

2 Which comes first, Christmas or Hanukkah?

3 When is New Year's Eve?

▶ Apply What You Learned

Make a calendar for the month of your birthday. Find out what other special days are in that month. Mark those days on your calendar.

159

Main Idea
Americans share many customs.

Vocabulary

custom

We Are Americans!

Our families have come from around the world to live in the United States. We share American **customs**, or ways of doing things. We also share customs from other countries. We are all Americans.

LESSON 5
Review

❶ **Vocabulary** What is a **custom**?

❷ Think about a custom your family has. Why is it important?

❸ Work with a partner to list customs you see in your community.

A Festival of Cultures

Get Ready

Americans come from many countries and cultures. Visitors to a festival can learn about the customs of other cultures. They can enjoy special dances, music, food, clothing, and crafts.

What to See

At this festival, people wear clothing that shows their different cultures.

Music is an important part of Mexican culture.

A Swedish woman makes a doll out of corn husks.

A man cooks plantains, which are like bananas. Plantains are a common food in Nigeria.

A Japanese woman dances with fans. Fans have been used in Japan for more than a thousand years.

Take a Field Trip

GO ONLINE

A VIRTUAL TOUR
Visit The Learning Site at
www.harcourtschool.com/tours
to take virtual tours of
other cultures.

READING RAINBOW

A VIDEO TOUR
Check your media
center or classroom library
for a video featuring a segment
from Reading Rainbow.

Visual Summary

Finish the chart. In the rectangle, write one more fact you learned. In the oval, write the big idea of this unit.

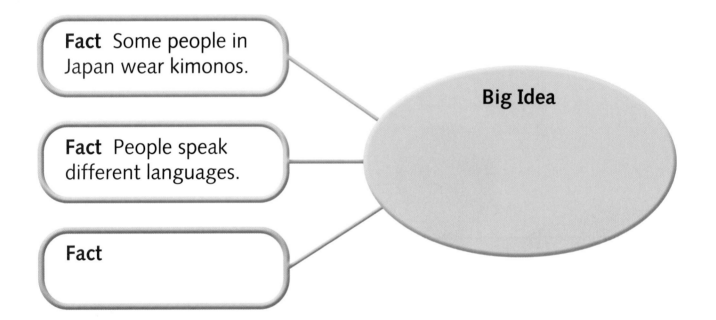

Fact Some people in Japan wear kimonos.

Fact People speak different languages.

Fact

Big Idea

THINK & WRITE

Make a Note Think about how your family and families you know meet their needs. Make a note of the different ways.

Write a Paragraph Describe similarities and differences in ways families meet each need.

Use Vocabulary

Write the word that completes each sentence.

1 My _____ at home is to be a helper.

2 Shaking hands is an American _____ .

3 Food, clothing, and shelter are all _____ .

4 A birthday party is a kind of _____ .

5 A group's _____ shows in its music, dance, and other arts.

role
(p. 134)

needs
(p. 138)

culture
(p. 143)

celebration
(p. 154)

custom
(p. 160)

Recall Facts

6 What are some ways people share their culture?

7 What does a map scale measure?

8 How are all Americans the same?

9 Which of these is a week-long African American holiday?

A Highland Games

B Kwanzaa

C Cherry Blossom Festival

D Chinese New Year

10 Which of these is the number of months in the year?

F 7

G 52

H 12

J 365

⑪ Three children want to play a game that only two can play. How would you solve this problem?

⑫ Why do you think people celebrate holidays from other countries?

Apply Chart and Graph Skills

October

Sunday	Monday	Tuesday	Wednesday	Thursday	Friday	Saturday
			1 Open House	2	3	4
5	6	7	8	9	10	11 Eleanor Roosevelt's Birthday
12	13 Columbus Day	14	15	16 Dictionary Day	17	18
19	20	21	22	23	24	25
26	27 Picture Day	28	29	30	31 Harvest Festival	

⑬ How many days are in this month?

⑭ When is Dictionary Day?

⑮ What happens on October 27?

⑯ On which day of the week is the Harvest Festival?

166

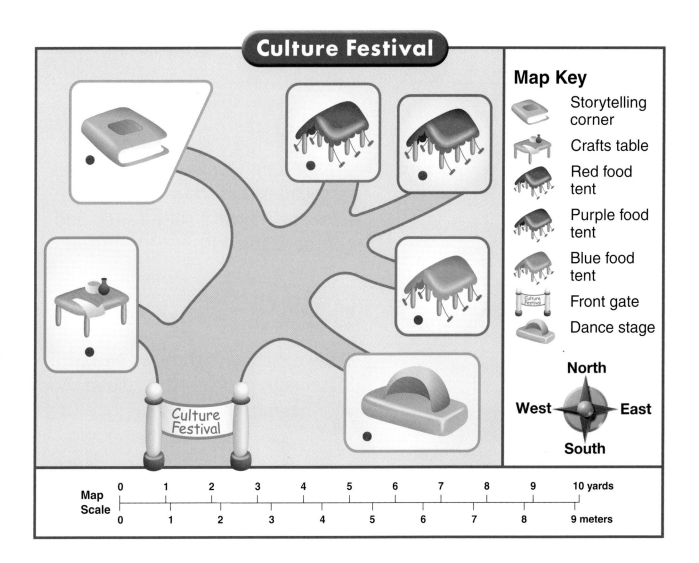

Culture Festival

Map Key

Storytelling corner

Crafts table

Red food tent

Purple food tent

Blue food tent

Front gate

Dance stage

North
West—East
South

Map Scale

0 1 2 3 4 5 6 7 8 9 10 yards

0 1 2 3 4 5 6 7 8 9 meters

17 How many yards is it from the storytelling corner to the crafts table?

18 How far is it from the purple food tent to the blue food tent?

19 From the front gate, in which direction is the dance stage?

20 What is south of the blue food tent?

167

Unit Activities

Visit The Learning Site at
www.harcourtschool.com/
socialstudies/activities
for additional activities.

Complete the Unit Project   Work with your group to finish the unit project. Decide how you will show people and their cultures in your book. Make the book cover.

Find Out

Look through magazines and books for pictures that show different cultures. Choose a culture, and find out more about it.

Share a Culture

Draw a picture that shows two of these ways people share culture. Add your page to the book.

- food, clothing, and shelter
- language   • music and dance
- art   • celebrations

Visit Your Library

Madlenka by Peter Sis. Neighbors share their culture with Madlenka.

Something's Happening on Calabash Street by Judith Enderle and Stephanie Jacob Gordon. People on Calabash Street share special meals.

Emeka's Gift: An African Counting Story by Ifeoma Onyefulu. Read about the Igala tribe in Nigeria, Africa.

Looking Back

A "cityscape"
ceramic clock, 1925

Looking Back

" Study the past if you would discover the future. **"**

—Chinese proverb

Preview the Content

As you read, think about important things that have happened in the United States. At the end of this unit, finish the chart. Show what happened in the correct order.

America's History

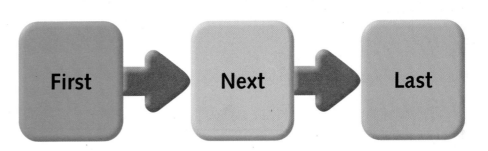

First ➡ Next ➡ Last

change To become different. (page 175)

season One of four parts of the year that have different kinds of weather. (page 175)

history The story of what has happened in the past. (page 178)

Our country old and new.

hero A person who has done something brave or important. (page 206)

technology New inventions used in everyday life. (page 210)

Four Generations

by Mary Ann Hoberman
illustrated by Russ Wilson

Sometimes when we go out for walks,
I listen while my father talks.

The thing he talks of most of all
Is how it was when he was small

And he went walking with <u>his</u> dad
And conversations that they had

About <u>his</u> father and the talks
They had when <u>they</u> went out for walks.

Think About It

1. Who are the people in this poem?

2. What are some things you talk about with your family?

Read a Book

Start the Unit Project

A Community History Quilt
Your class will make a quilt that shows the history of your community. As you read this unit, think about the stories people tell about changes in people and places. Look for new ways people learn to do things.

Use Technology

Visit The Learning Site at **www.harcourtschool.com/ socialstudies** for additional activities, primary sources, and other resources to use in this unit.

Time and Change

Main Idea
Things change
all the time.

Vocabulary

yesterday

today

tomorrow

change

season

You can talk about time in different ways.
Yesterday I got a new shirt. **Today** in
school I am learning about time.
Tomorrow I will go bowling.

today

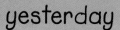

tomorrow

Things change over time. To **change** is to become different. We see things change in spring, summer, fall, and winter. Each of these times is called a **season**.

spring

summer

fall

winter

LESSON 1
Review

❶ **Vocabulary**   What are the four **seasons**?

❷ What are some things that have changed since the beginning of the school year?

❸ List some things you did yesterday and today. Then list things you would like to do tomorrow.

Use a Time Line

Vocabulary

time line

▶ Why It Matters

We need ways to show how things change over time.

▶ What You Need to Know

A **time line** shows when things happened and in what order. A time line can show days, weeks, years, or more. You read a time line from left to right. The things on the left happened first.

Samuel is born

Birthday party

Practice the Skill

1. Look at Samuel's time line. When did Samuel hit his first ball?

2. What happened last on the time line?

3. What happened when Samuel was two?

▶ Apply What You Learned

Make a time line of your school day.

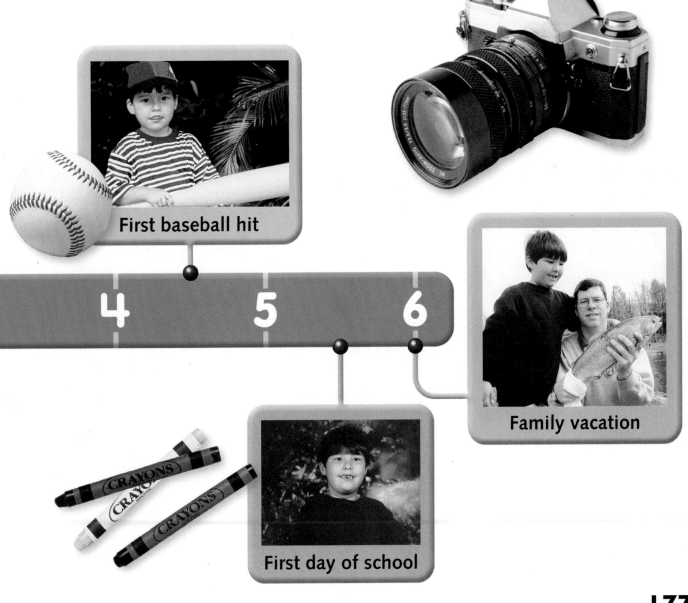

First baseball hit

4   5   6

First day of school

Family vacation

Main Idea
Families share their history through stories.

Vocabulary

history

Trace a Family History

Each family has its own history. **History** is made up of the stories people tell about what has happened.

Grandpa Ryan's photographs show our family history. He tells me about them.

"When I married your grandma, most photographs were black and white.

We celebrated your mother's first birthday with a party.

We were proud when your mother finished high school.

Your mother and father met in college. They married after they finished college.

This is the very first photograph of you."

Grandma Bridgette came to the United
States from Germany when she was
young. She likes to show me the things
she brought with her. She tells me a story
about each one.

"This clock has been in my family for many years. It was made by my great-great-grandfather. One day it will belong to you."

Clocks

People have kept track of time in many ways. Early people told time by where the sun, moon, or stars were in the sky. Some people used an hourglass. This tool is filled with sand. It takes exactly one hour for the sand to fall from the top to the bottom.

LESSON 2
Review

❶ **Vocabulary** What is a family's **history**?

❷ Why do you think people retell family stories?

❸ Interview a classmate to learn his or her favorite family story.

Use a Diagram

Vocabulary

diagram

▶ Why It Matters

One way to show a family history is with a diagram. A **diagram** is a drawing that shows parts of something.

▶ What You Need to Know

This diagram is called a family tree. It shows the parts of a family. You read the diagram starting from the bottom. As you go up the tree, you go farther back in a family's history.

▶ Practice the Skill

1 Look at the diagram of the family tree. Where can you find the youngest people?

2 Who are the people on the top row of the tree?

3 Who are Dad's parents?

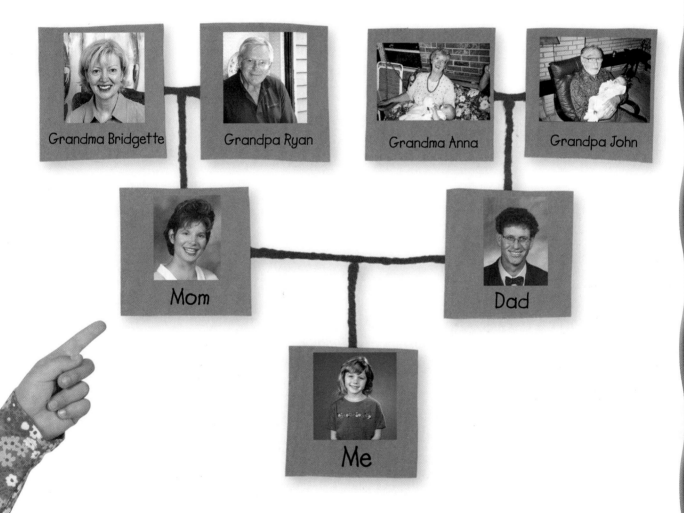

Grandma Bridgette Grandpa Ryan Grandma Anna Grandpa John

Mom Dad

Me

▶ Apply What You Learned

Make a family tree of your family or another family you know.

A Community History

Main Idea

Like people, places also grow and change over time.

Vocabulary

past

present

future

Every community and state has changed. Each place has its own history.

This is Wilmington, North Carolina, in the **past**, or the time before now.

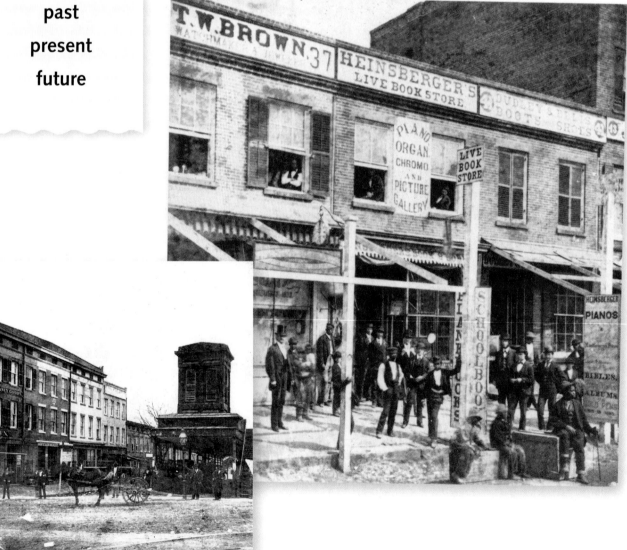

This is Wilmington in the **present**, or now.
There are more homes and new stores.

Wilmington will keep changing in the
future, or the time to come.

Leaders start communities
and help change them.

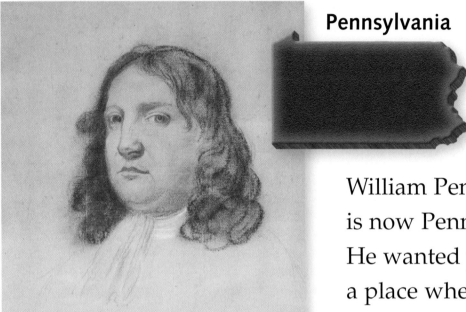

Pennsylvania

William Penn started what
is now Pennsylvania.
He wanted people to have
a place where they could
follow their own religion.

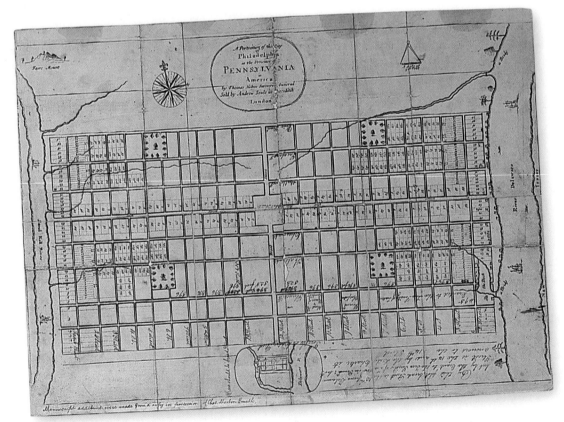

Philadelphia, Pennsylvania, 1683

James Oglethorpe wanted a place where people could start over. He and others from England started Savannah, Georgia.

Georgia

Stephen F. Austin brought Americans to live in Texas. Many Americans living in the East were looking for new lands farther west.

Texas

LESSON 3
Review

1. **Vocabulary** How can you learn about the **past**?

2. How has Wilmington changed from past to present?

3. Write a paragraph about something that has changed in your community.

Identify Cause and Effect

Vocabulary

cause

effect

▶ Why It Matters

Sometimes we need to explain why something happened. This helps us understand the past. It also helps us predict what will happen in the future.

▶ What You Need to Know

A **cause** is what makes something happen. An **effect** is what happens because of a cause.

cause

▶ Practice the Skill

❶ Look at the two pictures. What happens first?

❷ Does the effect happen before or after the cause?

❸ What is the effect?

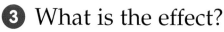

effect

▶ Apply What You Learned

People build new homes, schools, and stores in communities. What might be the causes for this? What might be the effects on people living there?

Main Idea
Many groups lived in North and South America before Columbus arrived.

Vocabulary

explorer

America's First People

Nez Perce

Mandan

Pomo

Hopi

Native Americans were the first people to live in North and South America. There were many groups, and each group had its own way of living.

Mohawk

Timucua

Explorers came from other countries to North and South America. An **explorer** is a person who finds out about new land. Christopher Columbus was an explorer who sailed from Spain in 1492. Columbus was looking for a new way to get to Asia.

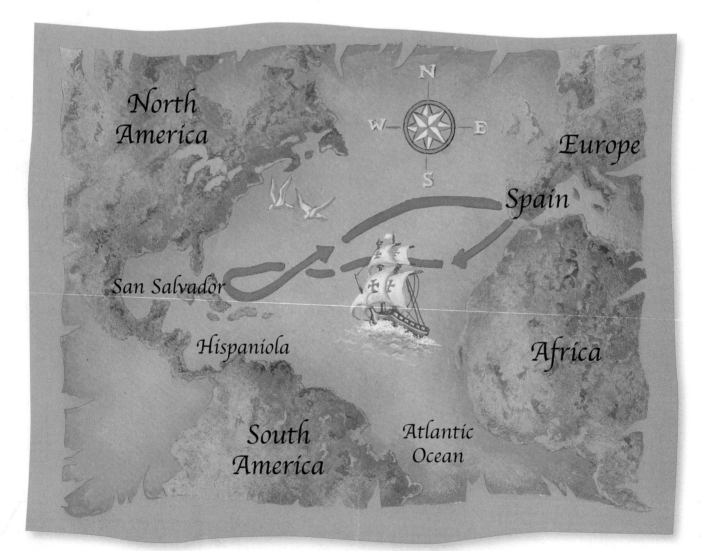

Columbus and his crew sailed for many days. Finally they landed on the beach of an island in North America. They met the Taino people who lived there.

When Columbus returned to Spain, he told people about the islands he had found. Soon many more people crossed the ocean to explore North and South America.

LESSON 4 Review

① **Vocabulary**   Which **explorer** came to North America in 1492?

② Why do you think explorers want to find out about new lands?

③ Read about an early Native American group. Write a short report telling how they lived.

Our Country's History

Main Idea
Our country's history is made up of many people and the things they did.

Vocabulary

settler

freedom

Long ago, people from far away began moving to North America. One group was the Pilgrims. They were **settlers**, or people who wanted to make a home in a new place. The Pilgrims sailed from England on a ship called the Mayflower.

 **FAST FACT** One child was born on the Mayflower during the Pilgrims' journey. His parents named him Oceanus.

Many native people lived in North America. The Wampanoags were the native people who lived where the Pilgrims landed. A Wampanoag man named Squanto lived with the Pilgrims. He showed them how to grow corn.

The Pilgrims were thankful for a good harvest. They celebrated with a great feast. Some Wampanoags came to this celebration. Today we remember this feast with a holiday called Thanksgiving.

More settlers came to North America. The land here belonged to England, and the people had to follow England's laws. They thought some of the laws were unfair.

On July 4, 1776, American leaders signed the Declaration of Independence. It told the King of England that Americans wanted to be free.

Americans fought a war for **freedom**, or the right to make choices. Today we celebrate our freedom with parades, picnics, and fireworks. This holiday is called Independence Day. It is our country's birthday.

Let freedom ring!

LESSON 5
Review

1 **Vocabulary** Who are **settlers**?

2 Describe the reasons we celebrate Thanksgiving and Independence Day.

3 Draw pictures to show how people celebrate these holidays.

Main Idea
We celebrate on holidays to remember our history.

Vocabulary

veteran

peace

Celebrating History

Thanksgiving and Independence Day are important American holidays. We celebrate our history on other holidays, too.

On Dr. Martin Luther King, Jr., Day, we honor a man who worked to make things fair for all Americans. He made speeches asking for equal rights for everyone.

Presidents' Day started as Washington's Birthday. It was a holiday to remember our first President. Now it is a day to remember the work of all our Presidents.

UNITED STATES POSTAGE
1732 WASHINGTON 1932
1

UNITED STATES POSTAGE
TAFT
4 CENTS 4

UNITED STATES POSTAGE
$5 CALVIN COOLIDGE 1923-1929 $5

UNITED STATES POSTAGE
ULYSSES S. GRANT 1869-1877
18 CENTS 18

· BIOGRAPHY ·

Abraham Lincoln 1809–1865
Character Trait: Self-discipline

Abraham Lincoln's family was poor. He could not go to school, so he studied at home. He became a lawyer and later President of the United States.

GO ONLINE

MULTIMEDIA BIOGRAPHIES
Visit The Learning Site at **www.harcourtschool.com/biographies** to learn about other famous people.

On Memorial Day we remember the people who died in wars for our country.

We are proud of the flag of our country. On Flag Day, people fly the flag from their homes.

On Veterans Day we think about the men and women who have fought in past wars. A **veteran** is someone who has served in the military. We give thanks for **peace**, a time of quietness and calm.

LESSON 6
Review

1 **Vocabulary** How have **veterans** served our country?

2 How do holidays help us remember history?

3 Choose one of the holidays you read about. Describe why we celebrate that holiday.

Follow a Route on a Map

Vocabulary

route

▶ Why It Matters

Routes on a map show us how to get from one place to another.

▶ What You Need to Know

Think about the school bus drivers who pick up children for school. They follow a route. A **route** is a path that leads from one place to another.

▶ Practice the Skill

1 Look at the map of the parade route. How is the parade route shown?

2 Where will the parade start?

3 In which direction will the parade go on Third Avenue?

4 What will it pass on Pine Street?

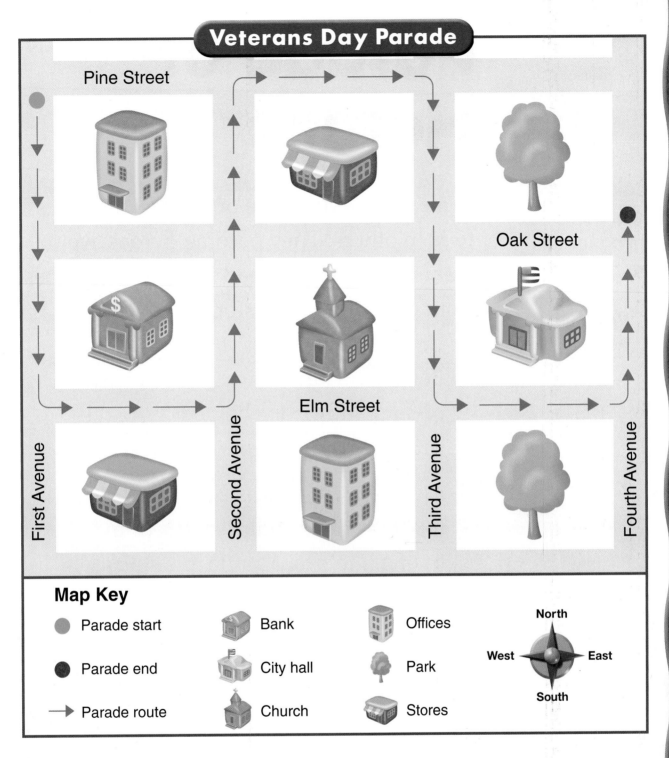

Veterans Day Parade

Pine Street

Oak Street

First Avenue

Second Avenue

Elm Street

Third Avenue

Fourth Avenue

Map Key

- Parade start
- Parade end
- → Parade route

- Bank
- City hall
- Church

- Offices
- Park
- Stores

North
West — East
South

▶ Apply What You Learned

Make a map of your community. Show the route you follow from home to school.

Practice your map and globe skills with the **GeoSkills CD-ROM.**

Parade of Heroes

Main Idea
People who do important things are heroes.

Vocabulary

hero

Some people do brave or important things to help others. They become **heroes** we want to remember. Read about these heroes from our country's history.

❶ **Benjamin Franklin** was a great leader of our country. He helped write the rules our country follows today.

❷ **John Paul Jones** was a sailor who fought for our country's freedom. In one important battle, his ships fought against larger ships and won.

❶

❷

❸

3 **Molly Pitcher** also fought for freedom. She gave thirsty soldiers water. She also helped the soldiers fire the cannon.

4 **Phillis Wheatley** wrote poetry. One of her poems is about George Washington. She believed he was a great leader.

5 **Sequoyah** was a Cherokee Indian. He wanted his people to be able to read and write their language. He made up an alphabet for them to use.

6 **Jane Addams** started a community center called Hull-House in Chicago. People who came from other countries could learn English and job skills there.

7 **Ida B. Wells** wrote about the ways African Americans were being treated unfairly. She wanted people to know the truth so things would change.

8 **George Washington Carver** showed farmers that planting peanuts made their soil better. He also found many uses for peanuts.

9 **Orville and Wilbur Wright** were brothers who were interested in flying. They worked together to make and fly one of the first airplanes.

10 **Sandra Day O'Connor** works for the government as a judge. It is her job to decide if laws are fair.

11 **Roberto Clemente** was a baseball player. He collected food and medicine to give to people who needed them.

LESSON 7
Review

1 **Vocabulary** Why are some people **heroes**?

2 What other heroes do you know about?

3 Compare two people from this lesson. Tell how the things these heroes did are the same and different.

Main Idea
Technology
has changed
many ways of
doing things.

Vocabulary

technology

transportation

communication

recreation

Everyday Life, Past and Present

When you wear clean clothes, ride to school, play a video game, or talk on the phone, you are using technology. **Technology** is all of the helpful inventions we use. Technology is always changing.

Household Tools

People are always making new tools to make daily chores easier.

· BIOGRAPHY ·

Thomas Alva Edison 1847–1931
Character Trait: Inventiveness

Thomas Edison wanted a better kind of light than candles and gas lamps. He made an electric lightbulb. At first only a few homes had this new technology. Now people around the world use electric light.

MULTIMEDIA BIOGRAPHIES
Visit The Learning Site at **www.harcourtschool.com/biographies** to learn about other famous people.

GO
ONLINE

Transportation

Transportation is ways of carrying people and things from place to place. People use transportation on land, on water, and in the air.

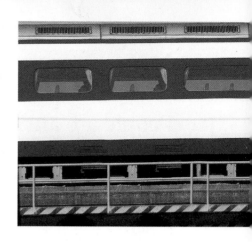

Airplanes today carry many passengers.

Bicycles have changed greatly over time.

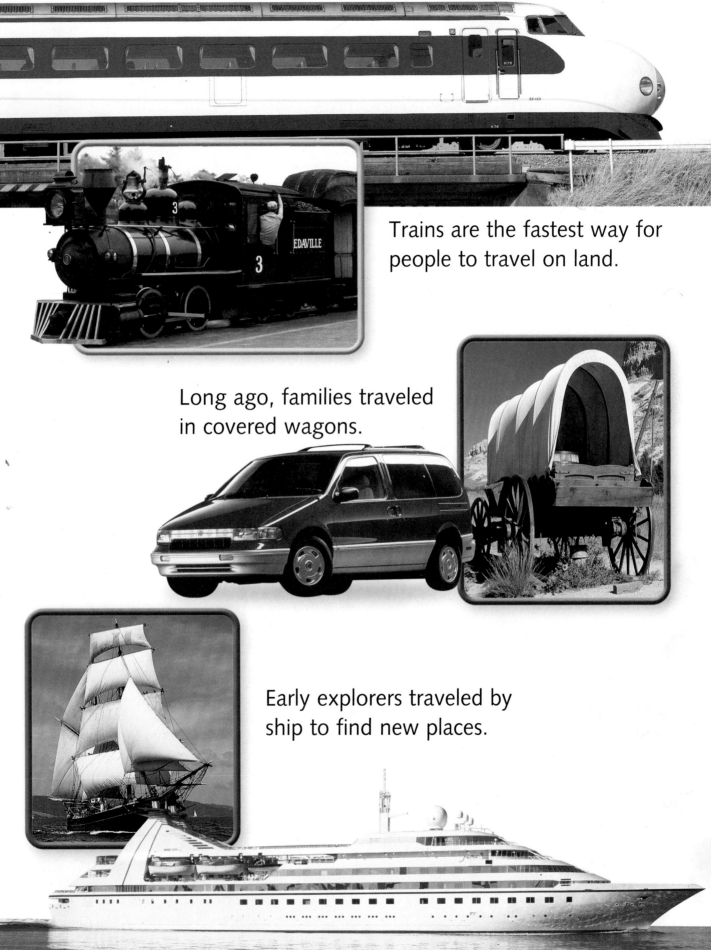

Trains are the fastest way for people to travel on land.

Long ago, families traveled in covered wagons.

Early explorers traveled by ship to find new places.

Communication

Every day, people talk or write to share their ideas and feelings. This sharing is called **communication** .

Communication Through History

Egyptian picture writing

Early handwritten book

Printed book

Pony Express

United States Postal Service

Facsimile machine

Stereoscope

Television

Satellite

Recreation

People like to relax in their spare time. **Recreation** is anything people do to have fun.

FAST FACT Long ago, people watched plays in large outdoor theaters. These theaters were made so people in the top rows could hear the actors.

LESSON 8
Review

❶ **Vocabulary**   How do you use **technology** at school?

❷ Describe how technology has changed transportation, communication, and recreation.

❸ Make a poster. Show more household tools that have changed the ways families do chores.

The Telephone

The telephone makes it easy for people to communicate. It was invented by Alexander Graham Bell. The first telephone call was from Bell to his helper in another room. Now we can use the telephone to talk with people around the world.

 How do you think these early telephones were used?

2 How has the telephone changed?

Activity

Choose another communication tool, such as the radio. Find out how it has changed over time.

Research

GO ONLINE

Visit The Learning Site at
www.harcourtschool.com/primarysources
to research other primary sources.

VISIT Old Sturbridge Village

Get Ready

Old Sturbridge Village is a good place to learn about the past. Actors dress up like the people who lived there more than a hundred years ago. They do the jobs those people did so visitors can see what life was like then.

What to See

1 Blacksmiths shape hot metal with hammers to make and repair tools.

2 Children play rounders in a field. Rounders is a game like baseball.

3 Children help their mother with home chores such as sewing.

4 Shoemakers use wooden pegs or thread to put the soles onto shoes.

Take a Field Trip

A VIRTUAL TOUR
Visit The Learning Site at
www.harcourtschool.com/tours
to take virtual tours of other
historic sites.

A VIDEO TOUR
Check your media
center or classroom library
for a video featuring a segment
from Reading Rainbow.

5 Review and Test Preparation

Visual Summary

Put these events in the correct order in the chart.

- Explorers came to North America.
- Pilgrims moved to North America.
- Native Americans lived in North and South America.

America's History

First → Next → Last

THINK & WRITE

Draw a Picture Think about a change that has happened in your family. Draw a picture of it.

Write a Letter Write to a friend or family member. Tell about the change shown in your picture.

Use Vocabulary

Give another example to explain each word.

	Word	Examples	
1	change (p. 175)	A new teacher at school	
2	season (p. 175)	Summer	
3	history (p. 178)	The Pilgrims give thanks	
4	hero (p. 206)	Abraham Lincoln	
5	technology (p. 210)	Electric light	

Recall Facts

6 What kinds of changes happen with the seasons?

7 In what year did Christopher Columbus sail to North America?

8 Why did Americans fight to be free from England?

9 Which holiday celebrates our country's birthday?

    A Presidents' Day   **C** Flag Day

    B Memorial Day   **D** Independence Day

10 For which of these is a bicycle used?

    F information   **H** communication

    G transportation   **J** history

221

Think Critically

11 How is our Thanksgiving holiday the same as the Pilgrims' Thanksgiving? How is it different?

12 How would your life be different if there were no telephones?

Apply Chart and Graph Skills

13 How much time is shown on the time line?

14 In what month was Theodore Roosevelt born?

15 Which two Presidents were born in the same month?

16 George W. Bush was born in July. Would you put his birthday before or after Thomas Jefferson's?

| JAN | FEB | MAR | APR | MAY | JUN | JUL | AUG | SEP | OCT | NOV | DEC |

Abraham Lincoln's Birthday

George Washington's Birthday

Thomas Jefferson's Birthday

Theodore Roosevelt's Birthday

17 On which bus route is the city hall?

18 Which bus route goes along Fifth Avenue?

19 Does bus route 2 pass through the west or the east part of town?

20 Which bus route could you take to go to the museum from Third Avenue?

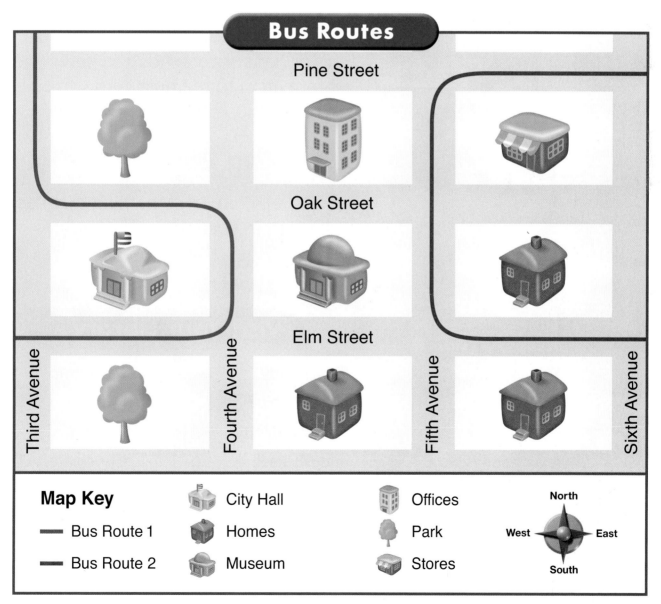

Bus Routes

Pine Street

Oak Street

Elm Street

Third Avenue

Fourth Avenue

Fifth Avenue

Sixth Avenue

Map Key

— Bus Route 1
— Bus Route 2

City Hall
Homes
Museum

Offices
Park
Stores

North
West — East
South

223

Unit Activities

Visit The Learning Site at
**www.harcourtschool.com/
socialstudies/activities**
for additional activities.

Complete the Unit Project Work with your group to finish the unit project. Decide how you will show the history of your community in your quilt.

Interview a Family Member

Write some questions you want to ask a family member about your community's history. Then interview the family member. Write down his or her answers. Add the new information to the quilt.

Showing Change

Draw a picture of something that has changed in your community.
• buildings • roads • places

Visit Your Library

 This Is the Turkey by Abby Levine. Max and his family prepare a Thanksgiving meal for family and friends.

 **On the Day the Tall Ships Sailed** by Betty and Michael Paraskevas. A bald eagle flies above New York City during an Independence Day celebration.

The Piano Man by Debbie Chocolate. A granddaughter retells her grandfather's stories about playing the piano for the silent movies.

Jobs People Do

A toy tool chest, 1910

Jobs People Do

❝ There is no
substitute for hard work. **❞**

—Thomas Edison, *Life*, 1932

Preview the Content

As you read, look for main ideas about jobs
people do. At the end of this unit, write
a sentence to summarize, or tell in a few
words, what the unit is about.

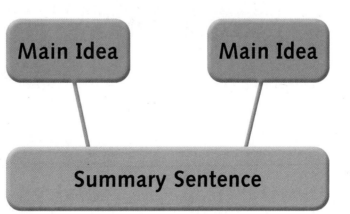

225

goods Things that can be bought and sold. (page 240)

services Work done for others for money. (page 242)

factory A building in which people use machines to make goods. (page 244)

market A place where people buy and sell goods. (page 258)

trade To exchange one thing for another. (page 268)

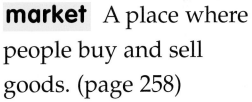

Rush Hour

by Christine Loomis
illustrated by Mari Takabayashi

Find out what jobs people do in this busy city.

228

Alarms are buzzing,
Day is dawning,
Sleepy people
Wake up yawning.

Showers splash,
Teeth are brushed,
Hair is combed,
Breakfast rushed.

Out their doors
Go moms and dads,
Lugging tools
Or books and pads.

Some alone,
Some with strollers,
Walkers, runners,
Readers, rollers,

Running, jumping
Onto trains,
Subways, buses,
Boats, and planes,

Taxis, bikes,
A car-pool van,
Cars of blue and red and tan.
Engines start up with a jerk.
People hurry off to work.

Horns go beep-beep, whistles blow,
Planes go fast, trucks go slow.
Trolleys sway, ferries rock,
Time keeps ticking on the clock.

Cars on side streets,
Trains on tracks,
Whizzing,
Zipping,
Clicky
Clack,

Rumbling,
Roaring,
Jiggling,
Jumping,

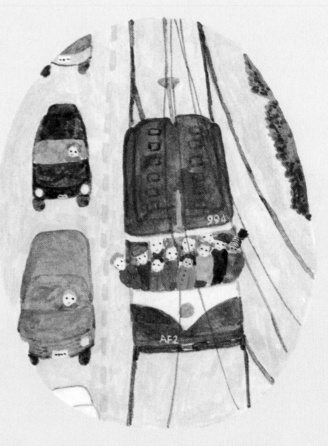

Left turn,
Right turn,
Backing,
Bumping.

Through the tunnels,
On the highways,
Over bridges,
Roads, and byways,
Down the river,
In the air,
People rushing everywhere!

In a blink
They disappear.
Trains are empty,
Tunnels clear.
Streets are quiet,
No more mobs.

233

People have begun their jobs.

235

When day is over,
Each job ends.
Workers wave
Good-bye to friends.

Then they race
To catch the trains,
Subways, buses,
Boats, and planes,
Taxis, bikes,
A car-pool van,
Cars of blue and red
and tan.

Down the river,
Underground,
Traffic creeping
Homeward bound.
Over bridges,
Roads, and byways,
Through the tunnels,
On the highways,

236

Right turn,
Left turn,
Backing,
Bumping,
Roaring,
Rumbling,
Jiggling,
Jumping,

Whizzing,
Zipping,
Clicky
Clack,
Cars on side streets,
Trains on tracks.

Horns go beep-beep,
Whistles blow.

Nighttime lights
Begin to glow.

Doors swing open.
Kids run fast.

Moms and dads
Are home at last.

Think About It

1. How are the workers in this book the same as workers in your community? How are they different?

2. Draw a picture of yourself doing a job you would like to do.

Read a Book

Start the Unit Project

Event Pamphlet Your class will make a pamphlet about an event at your school. As you read this unit, think about how people work together to complete a job.

Use Technology

Visit The Learning Site at **www.harcourtschool.com/ socialstudies** for additional activities, primary sources, and other resources to use in this unit.

Goods and Services

Main Idea
People depend on one another for goods and services.

Just like the people in <u>Rush Hour</u>, the people in your community are busy working every day. Some make goods. **Goods** are things that people make and sell.

pizza maker

furniture maker

potter

bakers

dressmaker

241

office worker

Other workers give services. **Services** are jobs that people do for others for money.

barber

mover

242

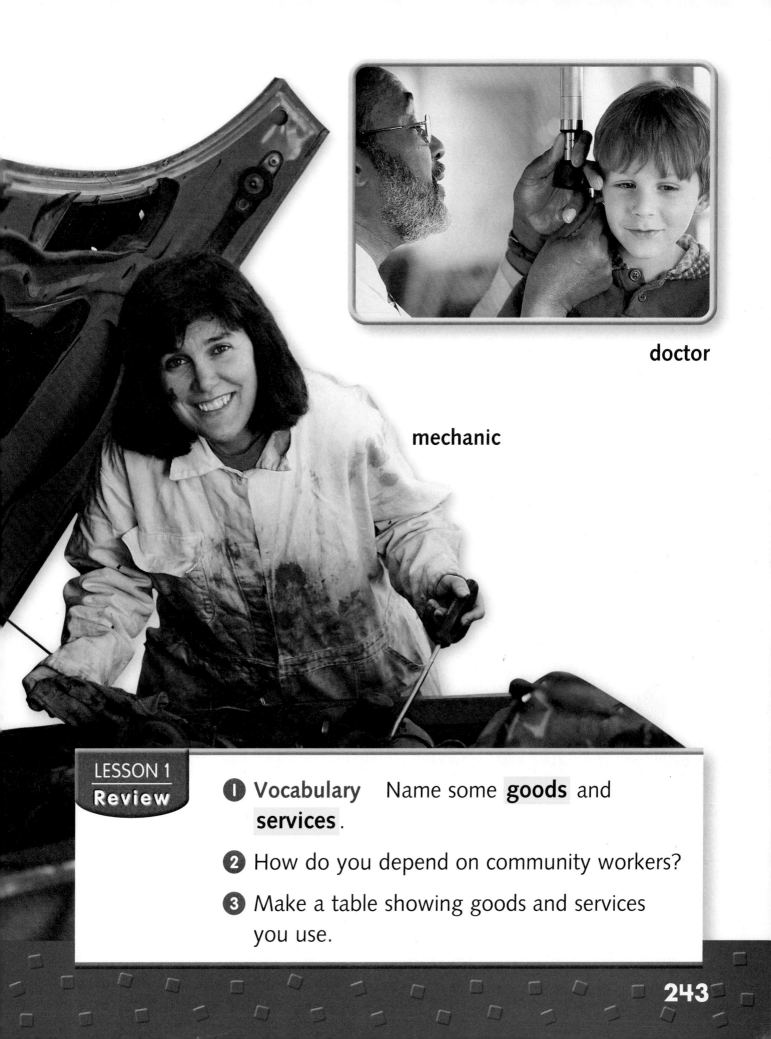

doctor

mechanic

① **Vocabulary** Name some **goods** and **services**.

② How do you depend on community workers?

③ Make a table showing goods and services you use.

Main Idea
People work together to make goods in a factory.

A Pencil Factory

Think about the pencil you use to write with. Resources are needed to make pencils. It also takes many people working together to make them. The pencils are made in a factory. A **factory** is a building in which people use machines to make goods.

GENERAL PENCIL COMPANY

Wood is needed for the pencils, so loggers cut down trees. Truck drivers take the logs to the factory. Later, foresters will plant new trees.

1

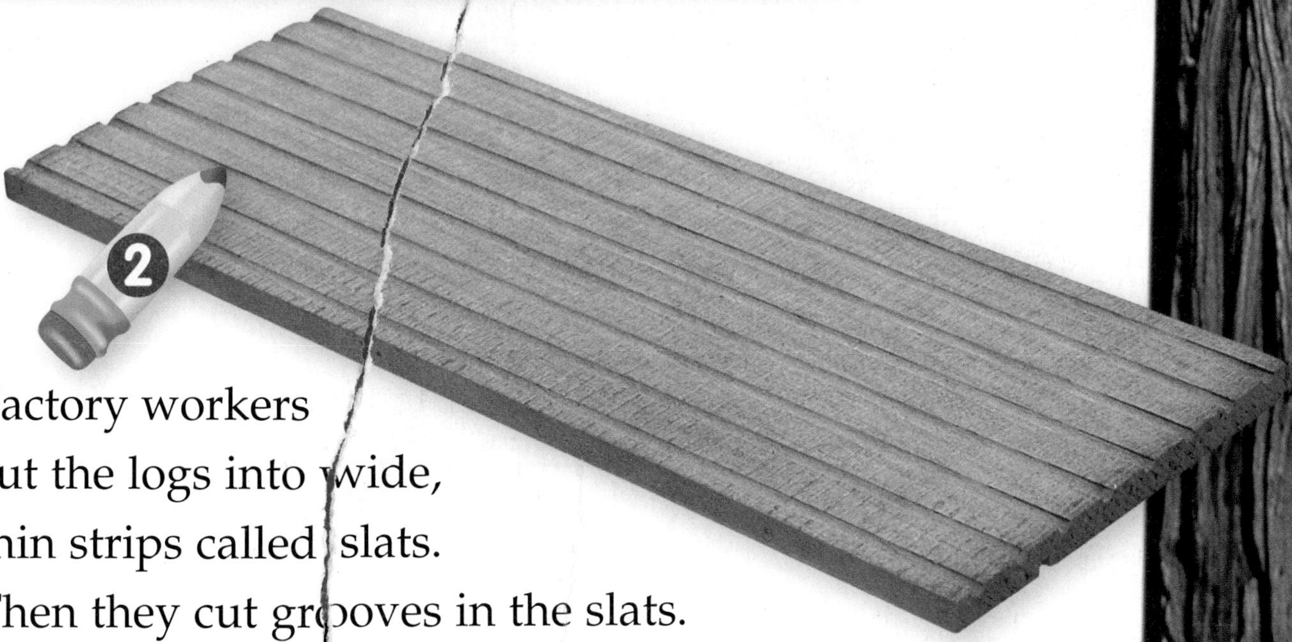

2

Factory workers cut the logs into wide, thin strips called slats. Then they cut grooves in the slats.

3 Workers put a pencil lead into each groove.

4 Then other workers glue an empty slat on top.

More workers cut the slat into separate pencils.

5

In another part of the factory, the pencils are painted.

6

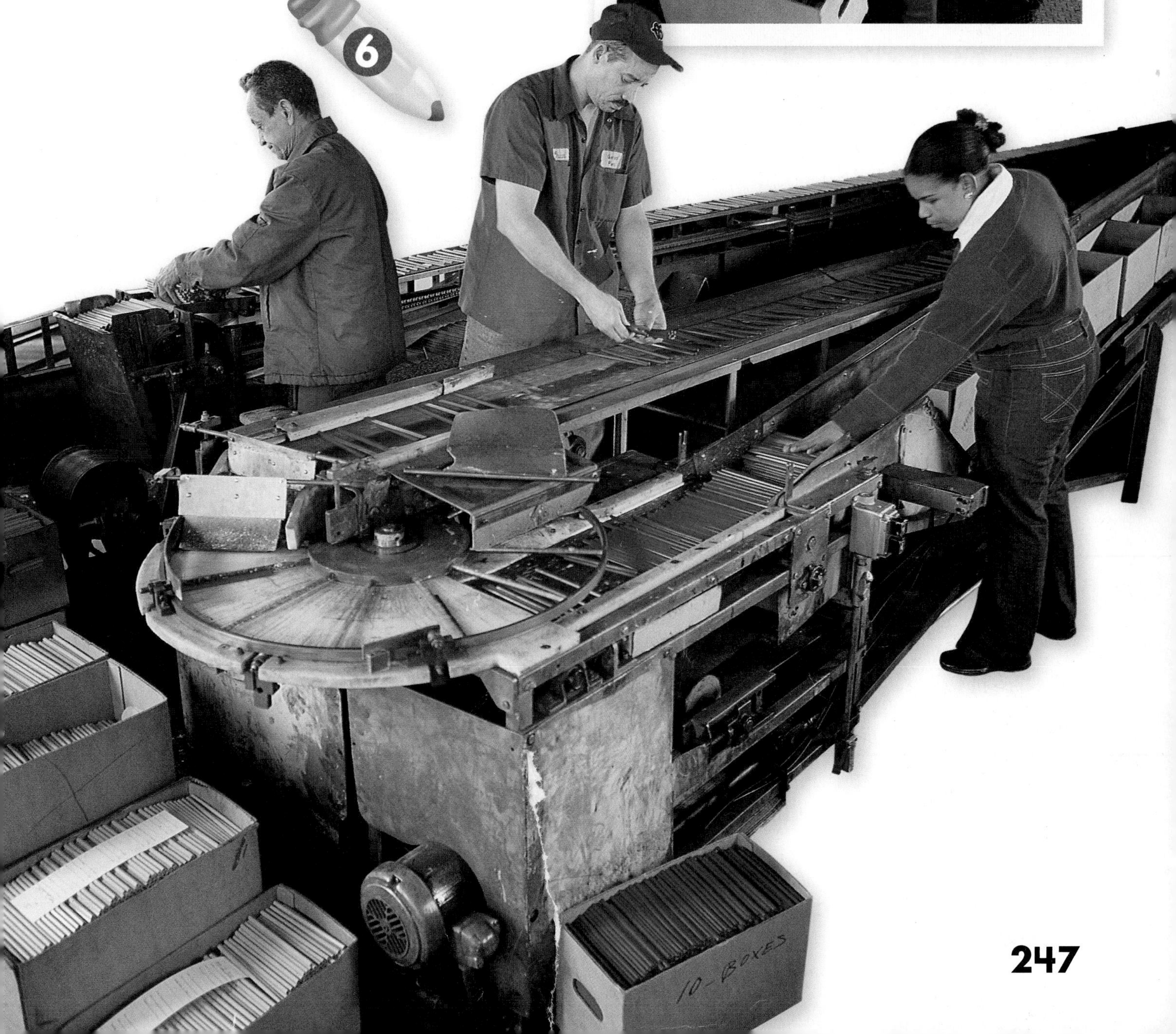

More workers add erasers to the pencils. At last the pencils are ready to be taken to stores and sold.

One of Mr. Taylor's jobs is to help people plan their gardens. Sometimes he is a volunteer at schools, helping children plant gardens. When he is a **volunteer**, he does not get paid for his work.

1 **Vocabulary** How do people use **money**?

2 Why might someone be a volunteer?

3 Find a picture of someone who is working. Write a sentence about the picture.

Jobs Change

Main Idea
The kinds of work people do and the ways they do them change over time.

Vocabulary

robot

New technology can change the way people work. It can make their work easier and help them work faster. Sometimes they may need to learn a new way of doing their job.

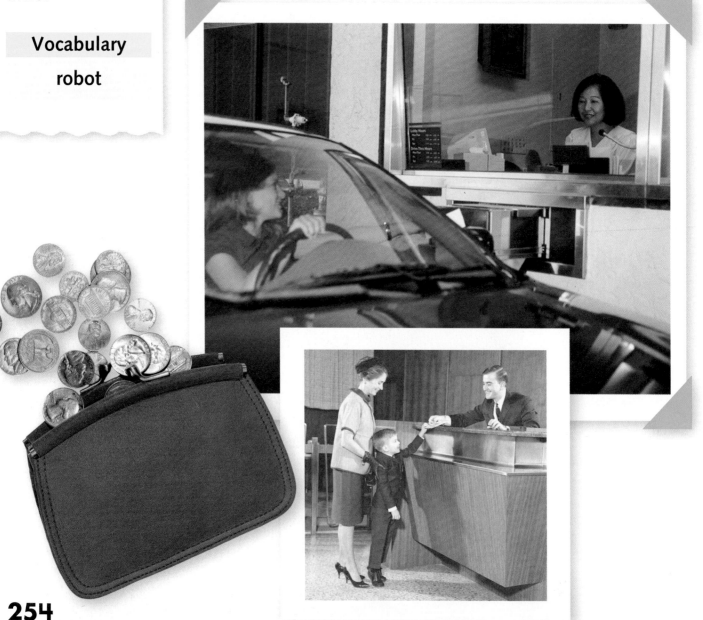

New technology has ended some old jobs. Grocery stores now have freezers and refrigerators. Workers are no longer needed to deliver ice and milk to people's homes. Special workers are no longer needed to run elevators.

RAILROAD BRAKEMEN
Rate $1.94¾ per hour; A-1 reference only. Apply 8 a. m. to 11 a. m. Monday through Friday at employment office, Union Railroad Co., 664 Linden Ave., East Pittsburgh.

New technology has made some new jobs. People use robots in factories. A **robot** is a machine that can do a job. It is run by a computer. Many office workers use computers, too.

LESSON 4
Review

1 **Vocabulary** How do people use **robots** at work?

2 Describe how technology has changed the way people work.

3 Design a machine that could help you do a job.

Buyers and Sellers

Main Idea
People can be buyers or sellers or both.

Our community has a large outdoor market. A **market** is a place where people buy and sell goods.

Today I have money to spend at the market. I am going to use it to buy a birthday present for my brother.

The sellers at the market use some of the money they earn to buy things they need. They **save**, or keep, some money to use later. They put this money in the bank. A bank is a business that keeps money safe for people.

Save for the future.

1 **Vocabulary** What do people do at a **market**?

2 What can you do with money you do not spend?

3 Draw a map of a market. Show six places shoppers might spend money.

Use a Bar Graph

Vocabulary

bar graph

▶ Why It Matters

Some kinds of information are easier to find on a bar graph. A **bar graph** uses bars to show how much or how many.

▶ What You Need to Know

The title of a graph tells you what it shows. This graph shows how many baskets of berries were sold at a market. The graph has rows that you look at from left to right. The picture shows the kind of berry. Each colored block stands for one basket of berries. The blocks show how many baskets were sold.

▶ Practice the Skill

1 Look at the bar graph. Which kind of berry sold the most?

2 Were more baskets of blackberries or raspberries sold?

3 Which kind of berry sold the least?

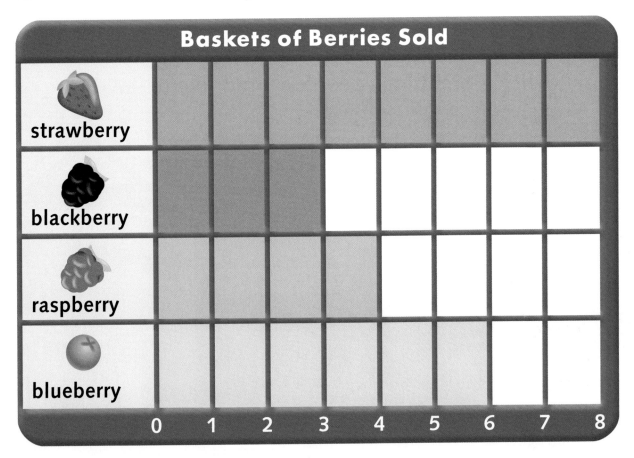

▶ Apply What You Learned

Make a bar graph to show the kinds of snack food the children in your class like to eat.

Wanting More or Less

Main Idea
People must make choices about what they want.

Vocabulary

wants

The Jacobs family is buying a new house. They need some things for their home. They also want some things, such as a garage, a backyard, and a fireplace. **Wants** are things people would like to have.

They know they should not spend all of their money. They will need some for food, clothes, medical care, and other needs. They budget, or plan, for what they need. They use some of what is left for things they want.

Monthly Budget

car - gasoline	70
clothing	150
food	600
house	950
medical insurance	200
other	200
savings	600
school supplies	40

LESSON 6
Review

❶ **Vocabulary** What are some **wants** people have?

❷ What must families think about before they spend their money?

❸ Cut out pictures from magazines or catalogs. Make a collage of things people want.

Make Choices When Buying

Vocabulary

scarce

▶ Why It Matters

Some things are scarce. When something is scarce , there is not enough. Money can also be scarce. Families cannot buy everything they want. They need to make choices.

▶ What You Need to Know

When you make choices, you must give up some things to get other things you want. You can follow these steps to make a choice.

Step 1 Decide if the choices are needs or wants.

Step 2 Think about what you would give up to get each choice.

Step 3 Make a choice.

▶ Practice the Skill

❶ Study the pictures to see how the Jacobs family is thinking of spending their money.

❷ Follow the steps. Decide what choice you think the family should make.

❸ Tell why you think the family should make that choice.

▶ Apply What You Learned

Shop with your family, and talk about the choices your family makes.

Trading with Others

Main Idea
People around the world depend on one another.

Vocabulary

trade

We trade for things that we want or need. When we **trade**, we give one thing to get another thing.

People trade with money.

JACK'S LEMONADE

People trade services.

People trade goods.

FAST FACT The 1909 Honus Wagner baseball trading card is so scarce, it sold for more than a million dollars!

Think about the goods you use every day. Many of these goods were made in other countries. People all over the world trade with one another.

MADE IN ITALY
HAND PAINTED

MADE IN CHINA

100% Cotton/Algodón
Machine wash cool with like colors
Use only non-chlorine bleach when needed
Tumble dry low
Lavar en lavadora con agua fría
con colores similares
Usar solamenté blanqueador sin cloro
Cuando se necesite
Made in India/Hecho en India
RN # 63232

Some goods are made in the United States with parts from other countries.

You can find out what countries the United States trades with. Just look at the labels in your clothes! You'll see that your clothes come from countries around the world.

Why are some clothing labels written in several languages?

100% COTTON/COTON/ALGODON
MADE IN U.S.A./FABRIQUE AUX E-U
HECHO EN LOS E.U.A.

X LARGE/T GRAND/
X GRANDE

MACHINE WASH WARM IN LIKE COLORS.
40°C LAVER A LA MACHINE A L'EAU TIEDE
100°F AVEC COULEURS SEMBLABLES.
LAVAR A MANO O EN LAVADORA CON
AGUA TIBIA CON COLORES SIMILARES.

ONLY NON-CHLORINE BLEACH.
AGENT DE BLANCHIMENT SANS
CHLORURE SEULEMENT.
SOLO BLANQUEADOR SIN CLORO.

TUMBLE DRY MEDIUM.
SECHER A TEMPERATURE MOYENNE.
SECAR A TEMPERATURA BAJA.

DO NOT IRON IF DECORATED.
NE PAS REPASSER SI DECORE.
NO PLANCHAR SI TIENE ESTAMPADO.

RN 15763   CA 21356

Philippines

Canada

China

U.S.A.

Japan

Mexico

271

People take their goods to market in many ways. Some goods do not need to travel far. In Thailand, small boats carry foods and other goods to markets nearby.

272

Some goods are sent to markets in other countries. Ships and airplanes carry goods from the United States to markets around the world.

People everywhere trade their goods to get the things they need and want.

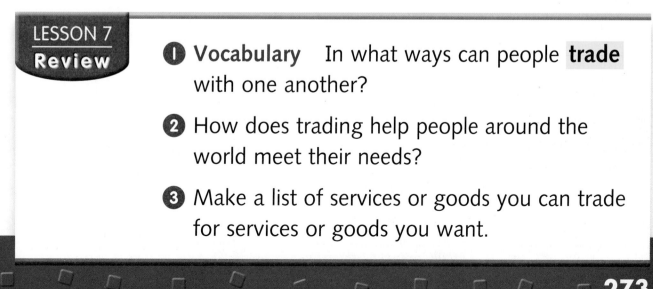

LESSON 7
Review

1 **Vocabulary** In what ways can people **trade** with one another?

2 How does trading help people around the world meet their needs?

3 Make a list of services or goods you can trade for services or goods you want.

VISIT

People at Work

In a community, people have different jobs. Many people work in offices. Others have jobs outside. Some people wear uniforms to work. People are working everywhere.

What to See

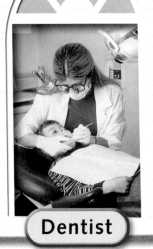
Dentist

Store clerk

Construction worker

274

Ballet teacher

Architect

Police officer

Taxi

Taxicab driver

Take a Field Trip

GO ONLINE

A VIRTUAL TOUR
Visit The Learning Site at
www.harcourtschool.com/tours
to take virtual tours of
other occupations.

A VIDEO TOUR

READING RAINBOW.
Check your media
center or classroom library
for a video featuring a segment
from Reading Rainbow.

275

Visual Summary

Write what you learned about the main ideas in this unit.

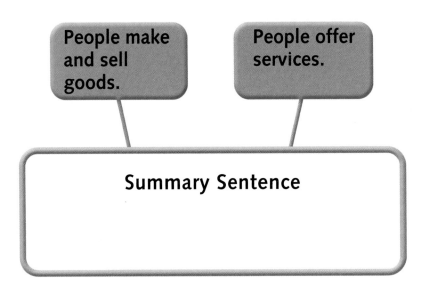

People make and sell goods.

People offer services.

Summary Sentence

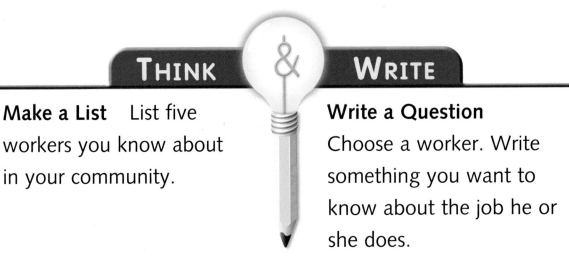

THINK & WRITE

Make a List   List five workers you know about in your community.

Write a Question
Choose a worker. Write something you want to know about the job he or she does.

Use Vocabulary

Fill in the blanks with the correct words.

People work together in a ❶ _____ to make ketchup, mustard, and soup. When the ❷ _____ are finished, they are put on trucks. The trucks take the goods to ❸ _____, where they are sold. People ❹ _____ money for goods at markets.

goods
(p. 240)
factory
(p. 244)
markets
(p. 258)
trade
(p. 268)

Recall Facts

❺ Name two services in your community that your family uses.

❻ What do people use to trade for goods and services?

❼ How does new technology change the ways people work?

❽ Why do people in one country trade goods with people in another country?

❾ Which of these workers makes goods?
    A baker   **C** barber
    B doctor   **D** bus driver

❿ Which of these is a want?
    F sandwich   **H** television
    G jacket   **J** house

Think Critically

11 What new jobs might there be in the future?

12 Why do you think people save money?

Apply Chart and Graph Skills

Patients	
Monday	🩺 🩺 🩺
Tuesday	🩺 🩺 🩺 🩺 🩺 🩺
Wednesday	🩺 🩺
Thursday	🩺 🩺 🩺 🩺
Friday	🩺 🩺 🩺 🩺 🩺

Key

🩺 = one patient

13 What does this picture graph show?

14 On which day did the doctor see the fewest patients?

15 On which day did the doctor see the most patients?

16 Did the doctor see more patients on Monday or on Thursday?

Where Ryan's Shirts Come From

	0	1	2	3	4	5	6	7
United States								
Mexico								
Taiwan								
Italy								

17 From which countries does Ryan have shirts?

18 From which country does Ryan have the most shirts?

19 Does Ryan have more shirts from the United States or from Taiwan?

20 How many of Ryan's shirts are from Mexico?

Unit Activities

 GO ONLINE

Visit The Learning Site at **www.harcourtschool.com/ socialstudies/activities** for additional activities.

Complete the Unit Project Work with your group to finish the unit project. Decide what information to put in your pamphlet.

Choose a Job

Choose one of the jobs needed to make the pamphlets.

- draw pictures
- write information
- fold pamphlets
- hand out pamphlets

Write an Announcement

Think about how to invite people to the event. Make your pamphlet colorful. Remember to tell what, when, and where.

Visit Your Library

Market Day by Lois Ehlert. See handmade items from around the world sold at a market.

Messenger, Messenger by Robert Burleigh. A bicycle messenger makes deliveries all over the city.

When I'm Big by Tim Drury. On a rainy day, a brother and sister imagine jobs they might have when they grow up.

For Your Reference

Biographical Dictionary
282

Picture Glossary
284

Index
303

Biographical Dictionary

The Biographical Dictionary lists many of the important people introduced in this book. The page number tells where the main discussion of each person starts. See the Index for other page references.

Addams, Jane (1860–1935) American who started Hull-House to help poor people in Chicago. p. 207

Aesop Greek who told fables that children still enjoy today. p. 150

Austin, Stephen F. (1793–1836) American who started a colony in Texas. p. 189

Barton, Clara (1821–1912) Founder of the American Red Cross. She was its first president. p. 69

Bell, Alexander Graham (1847–1922) American who invented the telephone. He also trained teachers to help people with hearing losses. p. 216

Bellamy, Francis (1855–1931) American minister. He wrote the Pledge of Allegiance in 1892. p. 41

Bethune, Mary McLeod (1875–1955) African American teacher. Her work gave other African Americans the chance to go to school. p. 15

Bush, George W. (1946–) 43rd President of the United States. His father was 41st President. p. 54

Carver, George Washington (1864–1943) African American scientist. His work helped farmers grow better crops. p. 208

Clemente, Roberto (1934–1972) Famous Puerto Rican baseball player who helped many people. p. 209

Columbus, Christopher (1451–1506) Italian explorer who sailed to the Americas. p. 194

Douglas, Marjory Stoneman (1890–1998) American writer. She worked to protect the Florida Everglades. p. 115

Edison, Thomas (1847–1931) American inventor. He invented the lightbulb and many other things. p. 211

Franklin, Benjamin (1706–1790) American leader, writer, and inventor. He helped write the Declaration of Independence. p. 206

Hale, Nathan (1755–1776) American hero who was captured by the British. p. 68

Houston, Sam (1793–1863) American who led Texas in its fight for independence. p. 69

Jefferson, Thomas (1743–1826) Third President of the United States. He was the main writer of the Declaration of Independence. p. 57

Jones, John Paul (1747–1792) Commander of the American Navy in the Revolutionary War. p. 206

King, Martin Luther, Jr. (1929–1968) African American minister and leader. He worked to win civil rights for all Americans. p. 200

Kwolek, Stephanie (1923–) American inventor. She found a way to make a cloth that is stronger than steel. p. 70

Lincoln, Abraham (1809–1865) 16th President of the United States. He made it against the law to own slaves. p. 201

O'Connor, Sandra Day (1930–) First female Justice of the United States Supreme Court. p. 209

Ochoa, Ellen (1955–) American astronaut. She was the first Hispanic female to go into space. p. 257

Oglethorpe, James (1696–1785) English settler who started the colony of Georgia. p. 189

Penn, William (1644–1718) English settler who started the colony of Pennsylvania. p. 188

Pitcher, Molly (1754?–1832) Nickname of Mary Hays McCauly. She brought pitchers of water to soldiers in the Revolutionary War. p. 207

Roosevelt, Eleanor (1884–1962) President Franklin Roosevelt's wife. She worked to make things better for the poor and for children. p. 70

Sequoyah (1765?–1843) Cherokee leader. He created a way to write the Cherokee language. p. 207

Wagner, Honus (1874–1955) One of the greatest baseball players in history. He played shortstop. p. 269

Washington, George (1732–1799) First President of the United States. He is known as "The Father of Our Country." p. 56

Wells, Ida B. (1862–1931) African American newspaper writer. She helped get laws passed for the fair treatment of African Americans. p. 208

Wheatley, Phillis (1753?–1784) African American poet. p. 207

Wright, Orville (1871–1948) and **Wilbur** (1867–1912) First Americans to fly a motor-powered airplane. p. 208

Picture Glossary

A

address
The numbers and words that tell where a building is. (page 84)

border

A line on a map that shows where a state or country ends. (page 52)

B

ballot
A piece of paper that shows the choices for voting. (page 58)

business

The making or selling of goods or services. (page 252)

bar graph
A graph that uses bars to show how many or how much. (page 262)

C

calendar

A chart that shows the days, weeks, and months in a year. (page 158)

cause
What makes something happen. (page 190)

citizen
A person who lives in and belongs to a community. (page 68)

celebration
A time to be happy about something special. (page 154)

city
A very large town. (page 50)

change
To become different. (page 175)

communication
The sharing of ideas and information. (page 214)

285

community
A group of people who live or work together. (page 46)

culture
A group's way of life. (page 143)

continent
One of the seven main land areas on Earth. (page 105)

custom
A group's way of doing something. (page 160)

country
An area of land with its own people and laws. (page 52)

D

desert
A large, dry area of land. (page 119)

I have a pet cat.

Her name is Snowball.

She is white.

detail
An extra piece of information about something. (page 8)

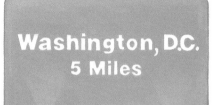

distance
How far one place is from another. (page 152)

diagram
A drawing that shows parts of something. (page 182)

Earth
Our planet. (page 104)

direction
The way to go to find something. (page 106)

effect
What happens because of a cause. (page 190)

explorer
A person who goes first to find out about a place. (page 194)

factory
A building in which people use machines to make goods. (page 244)

F

fable
A made-up story that teaches a lesson. (page 150)

fair
Done in a way that is right and honest. (page 11)

Fact The Liberty Bell cracked in 1835.

fact
A piece of information that is true. (page 66)

farm
A place where crops are grown and animals are raised for food. (page 108)

288

fiction
Stories that are
made up. (page 66)

freedom
The right of people
to make their own
choices. (page 199)

flag
A piece of cloth with
a special design that
stands for a country
or group. (page 62)

future
The time that is to
come. (page 186)

forest
A very large area of
trees. (page 109)

G

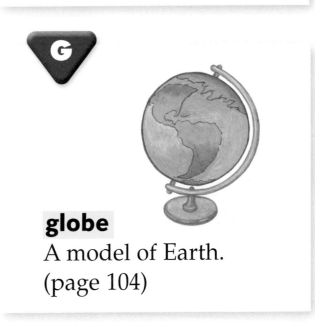

globe
A model of Earth.
(page 104)

goods
Things that can be bought and sold. (page 240)

group
A number of people working together. (page 12)

government
The group of citizens that runs a community, state, or country. (page 51)

H

hero
A person who has done something brave or important. (page 206)

governor
The leader of a state's government. (page 51)

hill
Land that rises above the land around it. (page 100)

history
The story of what has happened in the past. (page 178)

holiday
A day to celebrate or remember something. (page 154)

island
A piece of land that has water all around it. (page 101)

lake
A body of water that has land all around it. (page 99)

language
The words or signs people use to communicate. (page 132)

law
A rule that people in a community must follow. (page 46)

leader
A person who helps a group plan what to do. (page 48)

location
The place where something is. (page 18)

learn
To find out something new. (page 6)

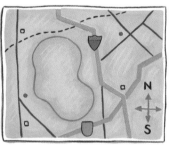

I have a pet cat.
Her name is snowball.
She is white.

main idea
What the information that you are reading is mostly about. (page 8)

litter
To leave trash on the ground. (page 115)

map
A drawing that shows where places are. (page 20)

map key
The part of a map that shows what the symbols mean. (page 96)

mayor
The leader of a city or town government. (page 50)

map scale
The part of a map that helps you find the distance between two places. (page 152)

money
The coins and paper bills used to buy things. (page 252)

market
A place where people buy and sell goods. (page 258)

mountain
The highest kind of land. (page 98)

N

needs
Things people must have to live. (page 138)

neighborhood
The part of a community in which a group of people lives. (page 94)

nonfiction
Stories that have real information. (page 66)

O

ocean
A very large body of salty water. (page 105)

P

past
The time before now. (page 184)

peace
A time of quietness and calm. (page 203)

picture graph
A graph that uses pictures to stand for numbers of things. (page 250)

pollution
Anything that makes the air, land, or water dirty. (page 114)

plain
Land that is mostly flat. (page 100)

predict
To say what will happen. (page 112)

point of view
A way of thinking about something. (page 146)

present
The time now. (page 186)

President
Leader of the United States government. (page 54)

R

recreation
The things people do in their spare time, such as playing sports or having hobbies. (page 215)

principal
The leader of a school. (page 14)

recycle
To use things again. (page 117)

problem
Something that causes trouble. (page 136)

religion
A belief in a god or gods. (page 144)

resource
Anything that people can use. (page 108)

river
A stream of water that flows across the land. (page 101)

responsibility
Something that a citizen should do. (page 73)

robot
A machine run by a computer to do work. (page 257)

right
A freedom. (page 72)

role
The part a person plays in a group or community. (page 134)

route
A way to go from one place to another. (page 204)

scarce
Not in good supply, or hard to find. (page 266)

rule
An instruction telling what must or must not be done. (page 10)

school
A place where people go to learn. (page 4)

save
To keep something, such as money, to use later. (page 260)

season
One of the four parts of the year that have different kinds of weather. (page 175)

services
Work done for others for money. (page 242)

shelter
A safe place to live. (page 138)

settler
One of the first people to make a home in a new place. (page 196)

solution
The answer to a problem. (page 136)

share
To tell others what we know or think. (page 7)

state
A part of a country. (page 52)

symbol
A picture or object that stands for something else. (page 20)

technology
New inventions that we use in everyday life. (page 210)

School Lunch Times

Class	Times
Mr. Turner	11:00 a.m.
Mrs. Rojas	11:15 a.m.
Mrs. Brown	11:30 a.m.

table
A chart that shows information in rows and columns. (page 28)

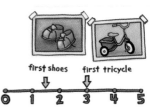

first shoes first tricycle

0 1 2 3 4 5

time line
A line that shows when events happened. (page 176)

teacher
A person who helps others learn. (page 14)

today
This day. (page 174)

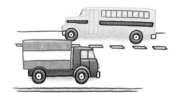

tomorrow
The day after today.
(page 174)

transportation
Ways of carrying
people and goods
from one place to
another. (page 212)

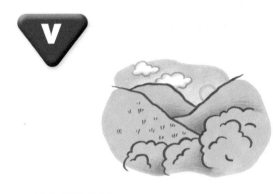

tool
Something a
person uses to do
work. (page 24)

V

valley
Low land between
mountains. (page 98)

trade
To give one thing to
get another. (page 268)

veteran
A person who has
served in the
military. (page 203)

301

volunteer
A person who works
without being paid.
(page 253)

weather
What the air outside
is like. (page 112)

vote
A choice that gets
counted. (page 58)

world
All the people
and places on Earth.
(page 30)

W

wants
Things that people
would like to have
but do not need.
(page 264)

Y

yesterday
The day before
today. (page 174)

Index

A

Abacus, 25
Addams, Jane, 207
Address, 84, 86–93
Aesop, 150–151
African Americans, 200, 208
Airplanes, 208, 212
Alamo, 61
Amazon rain forest, 120
"America" (Smith), 44–45
America, first people in, 192–195
American Red Cross, 69
Arkansas, 63
Art, 148
Artifacts, 1, 41, 81, 129, 169, 225
Astronaut, 257
Austin, Stephen, 189

B

Bald eagle, 60
Ballot, 58, 59
Bank, 260, 261
Bar graphs, 262–263
Barton, Clara, 69
Beliefs, 144
Bell, Alexander Graham, 216
Bellamy, Francis, 41
Bethune, Mary McLeod, 1, 15
Bicycles, 212
Boats, 196, 213, 272
Border, 52
Braille, 9
Brazil, 31, 118
Brooks, Gwendolyn, 74

Budget, 265
Burnham, Daniel, 75
Bush, George W., 54, 55, 222
Business, 252
Butterflies, 122–123
Buyers, 259, 265, 266–267

C

Cactus, 119
Calendars, 158–159, 166
Canada, 52, 143
Capitol Building, 45, 60
Carver, George Washington, 208
Cause, 190–191
Celebrations, 131, 154–157, 200–205
Change, 170
    jobs and, 254–257
    technology and, 210–217, 254–257
    time and, 174–175
Cherokee Indians, 207
Cherry Blossom Festival, 157
China, 121, 147, 249, 271
Chinese New Year, 156
Choices, 36
    buying, 266–267
    voting, 58–59
Christmas, 155
Cinco de Mayo, 156
Citizens, 43, 45, 71
    character traits of, 68–71
    honoring, 74–75
    portraits of, 68–71
    responsibilities of, 73
    rights of, 72, 73
City, 50

Clemente, Roberto, 209
Clocks, 181
Clothing, 138, 139, 140, 143, 148, 162
Columbus, Christopher, 194–195
Communication, 214, 216–217
Communities, 46, 47
   land and water in, 98–103
   law in, 42, 46–47
   leaders in, 48–51
   responsibilities of citizens of, 73
Community history, 173, 184–189
Constitution, 56
Continent, 82, 90, 105, 107
Countries, 42, 52
   houses and homes in, 118–121
   leaders of, 43, 54–57
Covered wagons, 213
Culture, 142–145
   book of, 133, 142–145, 168
   celebrations and, 154–157
   defined, 131, 143
   expressing, 148–151
   festival of, 162–163, 167
   museum of, 153
Custodian, 16
Customs, 131, 160–161
Cuyler, Margery, 84

Dance, 148, 163
Declaration of Independence, 198
Desert, 119, 121
Detail, 8
Diagrams, 182–183
Directions, on maps, 106–107, 126, 167
Distance, 152, 167
Doll making, 163
Douglas, Marjory Stoneman, 115
Drilling, 110

Eagle, 60
Earth, 92, 104, 105, 106–107
Edison, Thomas Alva, 211, 225
Effect, 190–191
Egypt, 32
England, 198
Everglades, 115
Explorers, 194–195

Fable, 150–151
Fact, 66
Factory, 227, 244–249
Fairness, 11, 70
Fall, 175
Families
   celebrations in, 154, 155, 156
   history of, 178–183
   interviewing members of, 224
   needs of, 138–141
Family tree, 182–183
Farm, 108
Festivals, 157, 162–163, 167
Fiction, 66–67
Firefighters, 34–35, 71
Flags, 43, 62–63, 65, 202
Food, 138, 140, 142, 146–147, 148, 163
Food server, 17
Forest, 109, 120
"Four Generations" (Hoberman),
   172–173
Franklin, Benjamin, 60, 206
Freedom, 198–199
   of religion, 72
   of speech, 72
"From Here to There" (Cuyler), 84
Future, 186

INDEX

Gas, 110
Geography, 119, 249
Georgia, 189
Germany, 30, 118
Globe, 104, 105, 106–107
Goods, 226, 240, 243
   trading, 268–273
   types of, 240–241
Government, 51
Governor, 51
Graphite, 249
Graphs
   bar, 262–263
   picture, 250–251
Groups, 2
   putting things into, 28–29
   working together in, 12–13

H

Hale, Nathan, 68
Hanukkah, 154
Hare and the Tortoise, The, 150–151
Heroes, 171, 206–209
Highland Games, 157
Hill, 100, 103
History, 170, 178, 181
   celebrating, 200–205
   of community, 173, 184–189
   of family, 178–183
   of Texas, 69, 189
   of United States, 192–199
Hoberman, Mary Ann, 172–173
Holidays, 154–157, 197, 200–203, 205
Homes, 118–121
Hopi Indians, 192
Hopkins, Lee Bennett, 4–5
Household tools, 211
Houses, 118–121

Houston, Sam, 69
Houston, Texas, 94
Hull-House (Chicago), 207

Idaho, 98
Independence Day, 199, 200
Indiana, 64
Indians, 132–133, 192–195, 197, 207
International Space Station, 257
Internet, 31
Inuit, 143
Inventiveness, 70
Island, 101
Israel, 144
Italy, 33, 121

J

Japan, 32, 143, 163
Jefferson, Thomas, 57, 222
Jobs, 234–236, 240–243, 252–257, 274–275
Jones, John Paul, 206

K

Kimonos, 143
King, Martin Luther, Jr., 200
Kwanzaa, 156
Kwolek, Stephanie, 70

L

Lake, 99
Land
   on maps, 102–103, 105, 127
   symbols for, 102, 103
   types of, 98–101, 119, 121
Language, 132, 145, 148
Law, 42, 46–47, 56, 115

INDEX

Leaders, 188–189
   of communities, 48–51
   of countries, 43, 54–57
Learning, 2, 6, 7, 30–33
Liberty Bell, 61
Librarian, 17
Lincoln, Abraham, 201, 222
Litter, 115, 117
Location, 18–19
Logs, 245
Loomis, Christine, 228–239

Main idea, 8–9
Mandan, 192
Map key, 96–97, 127
Map scale, 152–153, 167
Maps
   finding directions on, 106–107, 126,
     167
   finding states on, 52–53, 79
   following routes on, 204–205, 223
   of land and water, 102–103, 105, 127
   of neighborhood, 95–97
   symbols on, 20, 21, 39, 96–97,
     102–103, 127
   of United States, 53, 79, 89
   of world, 105
Market, 227, 258–261, 272, 273
<u>**Mayflower**</u> **(ship),** 196
Mayor, 50, 51
McGreene, Sheppard, 129
Memorial Day, 202
Mexico, 30, 52, 69, 119, 163
Milky Way galaxy, 93
Miller, J. Phillip, 129
Mohawk Indians, 132–133, 193
"Mohawk Way, The," 132–133
Money, 252, 253
   saving, 260–261, 265
   spending, 259–261, 265, 266, 267
   trading, 268

Motto, 64
Mount Rushmore, 61
Mountain, 98, 101, 103
Murals, 75
Museum, 153
Music, 148, 149, 163

Native Americans, 132–133, 192–195,
   197, 207
Needs, 130, 138–141
Neighborhood, 82, 94–97
Nez Perce, 192
Nigeria, 163
Nonfiction, 66–67
North America, 105, 107
North Carolina, 127
North Pole, 106, 107
Norway, 120
Nurse, 16

O

Ocean, 83, 105
Ochoa, Ellen, 257
O'Connor, Sandra Day, 209
Oglethorpe, James, 189
Oil, 110
Old Sturbridge Village, 218–219

P

Pakistan, 144
Parades, 204–205
Parks, 75
Past, 184, 189
Pasteur, Louis, 75
Patriotic symbols, 60–65
Patriotism, 68
Peace, 203

INDEX

Pencil factory, 244–249
Penn, William, 188
Pennsylvania, 64, 188
Philippines, 271
Picture graphs, 250–251
Pilgrims, 196–197
Pitcher, Molly, 207
Plain, 100, 101, 103
Plantains, 163
Pledge of Allegiance, 41, 62
Poetry, 4, 172–173
Point of view, 146–147
Poles, 106, 107
Police officers, 47, 275
Pollution, 114
Pomo, 192
Predicting, 112–113
Present, 186, 187
President, 43, 54–57, 222
Presidents' Day, 201
Principal, 3, 14, 15
Problem, 136
Problem solving, 136–137
Proverb, 169

Q

Quilt, 173, 224

R

Rain, 112, 113, 120
Rain forest, 120
Reading skills
    fiction and nonfiction, 66–67
    finding main idea, 8–9
    predicting, 112–113
Recreation, 215
Recycle, 117
Red Cross, 69
Reeds, 141

Religion, 72, 144
Resources, 83, 108, 111
    saving, 114–117
    types of, 108–111
Responsibility, 57, 69, 73, 115
Rights, 72, 73
River, 101
Robot, 257
Roles, 130, 134–135
Roof, 141
Roosevelt, Eleanor, 70
Roosevelt, Theodore, 222
Route, 204–205, 223
Rule, 2, 10–11, 38, 46–47
"Rush Hour" (Loomis), 228–239
Rushmore, Mount, 61

S

Savannah, Georgia, 189
Saving money, 260–261, 265
Scarce, 266, 269
"School Bus" (Hopkins), 4–5
Schools
    alike and different, 1, 36
    going to, 6–7
    long ago, 22, 24, 25
    map of, 20–21
    rules at, 10–11, 38
    today, 23, 26–27
    tools used in, 24–29
    workers at, 14–17
Scotland, 147
Seasons, 170, 175
Sellers, 260
Sequoyah, 207
Services, 226, 242, 243
    trading, 269
    types of jobs, 242–243, 274–275
Settlers, 196–198, 199
Share, 7

Shelter, 138, 139, 141
Ships, 196, 213, 272
Soil, 108
Solar system, 92
Solution, 136
Songs, 44–45, 65, 81
Sonoran Desert, 119
South Pole, 106, 107
Space station, 257
Special times, 154–157
Speech, freedom of, 72
Splendora, Texas, 86, 94
Spring, 175
Stamps, 201
States, 42, 52
    finding on maps, 52–53, 79
    flags of, 63
    leaders of, 51
    mottos of, 64
Statue of Liberty, 45, 61
Summer, 175
Sun Valley, Idaho, 98
Sweden, 163
Symbols
    for land and water on maps,
      102–103, 105, 127
    on maps, 20, 21, 39, 96–97, 102–103,
      127
    patriotic, 60–65
    of United States, 60–65

Tables, 28–29
Taino people, 195
Takabayashi, Mari, 228–239
Teacher, 3, 14, 15, 17
Teacher aide, 16

Technology, 171, 210, 215
    change and, 210–217, 254–257
    for communication, 214, 216–217
    household tools, 211
    for recreation, 215
    for transportation, 208, 212–213
Telephones, 216–217
Texas, 87, 94
    flag of, 63
    history of, 69, 189
    maps of, 87, 102–103
    motto of, 64
    song about, 65
"Texas, Our Texas," 65
Thailand, 272
Thanksgiving, 197, 200
Thatched roof, 141
Three Kings Day, 155
Time, 174–175
Time line, 176–177, 222
Timucua, 193
Today, 174
Tomorrow, 174
Tools, 24–29
    household, 211
    in past, 24–25
    present-day, 26–27
Trade, 227, 268–273
Traffic, 230–232, 236–238
Trains, 213
Transportation, 208, 212–213, 230–232,
    236–238
Trees, 109, 120, 245
Turkey, 147

Uniforms, 274

United States
  customs in, 160–161
  flag of, 62, 63, 65, 202
  foods in, 147
  history of, 192–199
  law in, 56
  leaders of, 43, 54–57
  maps of, 53, 79, 89
  motto of, 64
  Pledge of Allegiance to, 41, 62
  songs about, 44–45, 65
  symbols of, 60–65

Venezuela, 32, 120
Veteran, 203
Veterans Day, 203, 205
Viewpoint, 146–147
Village life, 218–219
Volunteer, 253
Vote, 58–59, 78

W

Wagons, covered, 213
Wales, 144
Wampanoag Indians, 197

Wants, 264–265
Washington, George, 56, 64, 207, 222
Washington Monument, 61
Washington State, 64
Water
  on maps, 102–103, 105, 127
  as resource, 111
  symbols for, 102, 103
  types of, 99, 101
Weather, 83
Weather prediction, 112–113
Wells, Ida B., 208
Western Hemisphere, 91
Wheatley, Phillis, 207
White House, 54, 55, 56
Winter, 175
Wood, 109
Work, 234–236, 240–243, 252–257, 274–275
Workers, school, 14–17
Working together, 12–13
World, 30–33, 105
Wright, Orville and Wilbur, 208

Y

Yesterday, 174
Yoruba (African group), 81

INDEX

309

For permission to reprint copyrighted material, grateful acknowledgment is made to the following sources:

Atheneum Books for Young Readers, an imprint of Simon & Schuster Children's Publishing Division: Cover illustration by Barry Root from *Messenger, Messenger* by Robert Burleigh. Illustration copyright © 2000 by Barry Root.

Curtis Brown, Ltd.: "School Bus" from *School Supplies: A Book of Poems* by Lee Bennett Hopkins. Text copyright © 1996 by Lee Bennett Hopkins. Published by Simon & Schuster Books for Young Readers.

Marc Brown Studios: From *Arthur Meets the President* by Marc Brown. Copyright © 1991 by Marc Brown. Published by Little, Brown and Company (Inc.).

Charlesbridge Publishing, Inc.: Cover illustration by Ralph Masiello from *The Flag We Love* by Pam Muñoz Ryan. Illustration copyright © 1996 by Ralph Masiello.

Children's Press, a Division of Grolier Publishing: From *George Washington: First President of the United States* by Carol Greene. Copyright © 1991 by Childrens Press®, Inc.

Chronicle Books, San Francisco: Cover illustration by Donna Ingemanson from *Something's Happening on Calabash Street* by Judith Ross Enderle and Stephanie Jacob Gordon. Illustration copyright © 2000 by Donna Ingemanson.

Cobblehill Books, an affiliate of Dutton Children's Books, a division of Penguin Putnam Inc.: Cover photographs from *Emeka's Gift: An African Counting Story* by Ifeoma Onyefulu. Photographs copyright © 1995 by Ifeoma Onyefulu.

Crown Children's Books, a division of Random House, Inc.: Cover illustration by Annette Cable from *Me on the Map* by Joan Sweeney. Illustration copyright © 1996 by Annette Cable.

Farrar, Straus and Giroux, LLC: Cover illustration from *Madlenka* by Peter Sis. Copyright © 2000 by Peter Sis.

Harcourt, Inc.: Cover illustration from *Market Day* by Lois Ehlert. Copyright © 2000 by Lois Ehlert. Cover illustration from *Check It Out! The Book About Libraries* by Gail Gibbons. Copyright © 1985 by Gail Gibbons.

HarperCollins Publishers: Cover illustration by Diane Greenseid from *Get Up and Go!* by Stuart J. Murphy. Illustration copyright © 1996 by Diane Greenseid.

Holiday House, Inc.: Cover illustration from *First Day, Hooray!* by Nancy Poydar. Copyright © 1999 by Nancy Poydar.

Henry Holt and Company, LLC: From *Here to There* by Margery Cuyler, illustrated by Yu Cha Pak. Text copyright © 1999 by Margery Cuyler; illustrations copyright © 1999 by Yu Cha Pak.

Houghton Mifflin Company: Cover illustration by Arthur Geisert from *Haystack* by Bonnie Geisert. Illustration copyright © 1995 by Arthur Geisert. From *Rush Hour* by Christine Loomis, illustrated by Mari Takabayashi. Text copyright © 1996 by Christine Loomis; illustrations copyright © 1996 by Mari Takabayashi.

Little, Brown and Company (Inc.): "Four Generations" from *Fathers, Mothers, Sisters, Brothers: A Collection of Family Poems* by Mary Ann Hoberman. Text copyright © 1991 by Mary Ann Hoberman.

The Millbrook Press: Cover illustration by Anca Hariton from *Compost! Growing Gardens from Your Garbage* by Linda Glaser. Illustration copyright © 1996 by Anca Hariton.

Scholastic Inc.: Cover illustration by Nila Aye from *When I'm Big* by Tim Drury. Illustration copyright © 1999 by Nila Aye. Published by Orchard Books, an imprint of Scholastic Inc.

SeaStar Books, a division of North-South Books, Inc., New York: Cover illustration from *The Inside-Outside Book of Washington, D.C.* by Roxie Munro. Copyright © 1987, 2001 by Roxie Munro.

Simon & Schuster Books for Young Readers, an imprint of Simon & Schuster Children's Publishing Division: Cover illustration by Michael P. Paraskevas from *On the Day the Tall Ships Sailed* by Betty Paraskevas. Illustration copyright © 2000 by Michael P. Paraskevas.

Walker and Company: Cover illustration by Eric Velasquez from *The Piano Man* by Debbi Chocolate. Illustration copyright © 1998 by Eric Velasquez.

Albert Whitman & Company: Cover illustration by Paige Billin-Frye from *This Is the Turkey* by Abby Levine. Illustration copyright © 2000 by Paige Billin-Frye. Cover illustration by DyAnne DiSalvo-Ryan from *If I Were President* by Catherine Stier. Illustration copyright © 1999 by DyAnne DiSalvo-Ryan.

PHOTO CREDITS:
KEY: (T)-TOP; (B)-BOTTOM; (L)-LEFT; (R)-RIGHT; (C)-CENTER; (BG)-BACKGROUND; (FG)-FOREGROUND

FRONT TITLE PAGE

Front Side: (fg) Minden Pictures; (bg) Don Mason/Corbis Stock Market; Back Side: (bg) Don Mason/Corbis Stock Market

TITLE PAGE AND TABLE OF CONTENTS:

i (fg) Shelburne Museum; i (bg) Doug Armand/Stone; ii (bl) Shelburne Museum; iv (cl) Shelburne Museum: v (tl) Newlab; viii (tl) Erich Lessing/Art Resource; ix (tl) Smithsonian Institution

UNIT 1:

Opener: (fg) Shelburne Museum; 1 (tc) Shelburne Museum; 2 (cr) Ellen Senisi/The Image Works, Inc.; 3 (tr) Superstock; 3 (bl) Bob Daemmrich/Stock, Boston; 9 (tl) J.C. Carton/Bruce Coleman, Inc.; 14 (b) Bob Daemmrich Photography; 15 (t) Jim Pickerell/Stock Connection/PictureQuest; 15 (b) Gordon Parks/Hulton/Archive Photos; 16 (t) L. O'Shaughnessy/H. Armstrong Roberts; 17 (t) Bob Daemmrich Photography; 18 (b) Peter Cade/Stone; 22 (c) Jeff Greenberg/Stock, Boston; 22 (c) Mark E. Gibson Photography; 23 (c) Richard T. Nowitz; 23 (bl) West Sedona School; 23 (br) James Marshall/The Image Works; 24 (t,c & bl) Blackwell History of Education Museum; 25 (b) Jack McConnell/McConnell & McNamara; 25 (tl) Gloria Rejune Adams/Old School Square; 26 (tl) Brent Jones/Stock, Boston; 26 (br) Michael Newman/PhotoEdit/PictureQuest; 28 (t) Blackwell History of Education Museum; 29 (cl, bl & tl) Blackwell History of Education Museum; 29 (bcl) Gloria Rejune Adams/Old School Square; 30 (cr) G. Popov/Sovfoto/Eastfoto/PictureQuest; 30 (bl) Bob Daemmrich Photography/Stock, Boston; 31 (br) Jay Ireland & Georgienne E. Bradley/Bradleyireland.com; 31(cr) Nicholas DeVore, III/Bruce Coleman, Inc.; 31(cl) Sheila McKinnon/Mira; 32 (t) Victor Englebert; 32 (bl) Burbank/The Image Works; 33 (c) D. Donadoni/Bruce Coleman, Inc.; 34-35 (all) Photopia

UNIT 2

Opener: (fg) Newlab; (bg) Robert Frerck/Odyssey Productions, Chicago; 41 (tc) Newlab; 42 (tl) David Young-Wolff/PhotoEdit/PictureQuest; 43 (tl) Reuters NewMedia/Corbis; 43 (bl) B. Daemmrich/The Image Works; 43 (cr) John Henry Williams/Bruce Coleman, Inc.; 46 (c) Alan Schein/Corbis Stock Market; 46 (br) DiMaggio/Kalish/Corbis Stock Market; 46 (cr) Joe Sohm/Pictor; 47 (c) ©Diane M. Meyer; 49 (t) Ken Chernus/FPG International; 49 (cl) PhotoDisc/Getty Images; 50-51 (all) David R. Frazier; 52 (br) Michael Hubrich/Photo Researchers; 52 (bg) Corel Collection, 1993; 54 (b) MIA/TimePix; 55 (t) Time For Kids Magazine; 55 (bl) Reuters/TimePix; 55 (br) Tim Sloan/Corbis; 55 (cr) Robert Essel/Corbis Stock Market; 56 (bc) Peggy and Ronald Barnett/Corbis Stock Market; 56 (cr) Visions of America; 60 (c) Frank Oberle/Stone; 60 (b) Phil Degginger/Color-Pic, Inc.; 61 (tl) Kunio Owaki/Corbis Stock Market; 61 (tr) Ed Wheeler/Corbis Stock Market; 61 (bl) B. Bachmann/The Image Works, Inc.; 61 (br) Joe Sohm/Visions of America; 61(cl) D. Boone/Corbis; 63 (t) Joe Sohm/Visions of America; 63 (cl) Bob Daemmrich/The Image Works, Inc.; 64 (b) Joe Sohm/Visions of America; 65 (cl) The Granger Collection; 66 (t) Grolier Publishing; 66 (b) Grolier Publishing; 68 (bl) The Antiquarian & Landmarks Society; 68 (cr) Joe Sohm/Visions of America; 69 (tl) Hulton Archive; 69 (bl) National Archives; 69 (br) Joe Sohm/Visions of America; 70 (t) Bettmann/Corbis; 70 (bl) Courtesy of DuPont; 70 (br) Color-Pic, Inc./E.R. Degginger; 71 (c) Anton Oparin/Corbis SABA; 72 (bl) PictureQuest; 72 (br) Bob Daemmrich/Stock, Boston/PictureQuest; 73 (tl) Michael Newman/PhotoEdit; 73 (cr) Photodisc; 74 (b) Larry Evans/Black Star; 74 (cr) Bettmann/Corbis; 75 (c) Larry Evans/Black Star; 75 (tc) Public Art Program/Chicago Cultural Center; 75 (tr) Chicago Historical Society; 75 (bl) Todd Buchanan/Black Star; 75 (cr) Hulton-Deutsch Collection/Corbis

UNIT 3

Opener: (bg) Mark E. Gibson; 82 (tl) Richard Pasley/Stock, Boston; 82 (br) Nigel Press/Stone; 83 (tl) Buddy Mays/Travel Stock; 83 (bl) W. Perry Conway/Corbis; 83 (br) R. Walker/H. Armstrong Roberts, Inc.; 94 (b) Bob Daemmrich Photography; 96 (b) Robert Winslow/The Viesti Collection; 98 (bc) Superstock; 98-99 (bg) Superstock; 99 (b) Joseph R. Melanson/Aerials Only Gallery/Aero Photo; 99 (cl) U. S. Postal Services; 100 (both) Superstock; 101 (tc) T. Dickinson/The Image Works; 101 (tr) U.S. Postal Services; 101 (cr)Robert Winslow/The Viesti Collection; 102-103 (b) Dick Dietrich; 108 (bl) Bruce Hands/Stone; 108-109 (bg) John Lawrence/Stone; 109 (tr) Fred Habegger/Grant Heilman Photography; 109 (cr & br) B. Daemmrich/The Image Works; 110 (bl) Mark E. Gibson Photography; 111 (tr) David Young-Wolf/PhotoEdit; 111 (br) Bob Daemmrich/The Image Works; 111 (bg) Jan Butchofsky-Houser/Houserstock; 111 (cl) Jim Nilsen/Stone; 112 (b) A. & J. Verkaik/Corbis Stock Market; 113 (c) Larry Lefever/Grant Heilman Photography; 114 (b) Dan Guravich/Corbis; 114-115 (bg) Randy

Wells Photography; 115 (cr) Kevin Fleming/Corbis; 116 (tr) Geri Engberg Photography; 117 (cl) Mark E. Gibson Photography; 118 (c & br) Superstock; 118 (bg) Buddy Mays/Travel Stock Photography; 119 (tr) W. Jacobs/Art Directors & TRIP Photo Library; 119 (tr) Jay Ireland & Georgienne E. Bradley/Bradleyireland.com; 119 (bl) Inger Hogstrom/Danita Delimont, Agent; 119 (cl) K. Rice/H. Armstrong Roberts, Inc.; 120 (b) Superstock; 120 (tr) Siede Preis/PhotoDisc/PictureQuest; 121 (tc) Superstock; 121 (tr) Sami Sarkis/Getty Images/PhotoDisc; 121 (bc) PhotoDisc/Getty Images; 121 (cl) Wolfgang Kaehler Photography; 122 (tr) Ian Adams/Garden Image; 122 (bl) Sara Demmons; 122 (cr) Laurie Dove/Garden Image; 123 (tr) Phillip Roullard/Garden Image; 123 (tl, bl & cl) Judith Lindsey; 123 (cr) Woodbridge Williams/Garden Image

UNIT 4

30 (tl) Norbert Schafer/Corbis Stock Market; 131 (tl) Lee Snider/The Image Works; 131 (tr) Bachmann/Unicorn Stock Photos; 131 (bl) Bob Daemmrich/Stock, Boston; 132 (bl) Marilyn "Angel" Wynn/Nativestock.com; 132 (br & t) Melanie Weiner Photography; 133 (c) Photodisc; 140 (tr) H.Thomas III/Unicorn Stock Photos; 140 (bl) Bob Daemmrich/The Image Works, Inc.; 140 (br) Dave Bartruf/Corbis; 140 (cl) John Elk III; 141 (b & tr) Topham/The Image Works; 141 (tl) Eric Crichton/Bruce Coleman, Inc.; 142 (cr) Ted Streshinsky/Corbis; 143 (tr) Superstock; 143 (bc) Momatiuk Eastcott/The Image Works; 143 (cl) Susan Lapides/Woodfin Camp & Associates; 144 (tl) Hanan Isachar/www.holylandimges.com; 144 (tr) Christine Osborne Pictures; 144 (bc) Macduff Everton/The Image Works; 144 (br) David R. Frazier; 148 (bl)The Newark Museum/Art Resource, NY; 148 (cr) Corbis; 149 (t) C Squared Studios/PhotoDisc/PictureQuest; 149 (bl) Bowers Museum of Cultural Arts/Corbis; 149 (br) Lawrence Migdale; 149 (cr) Mimmo Jodice/Corbis; 150 (cl) The University of Southern Mississippi; 151 (cl) Courtesy of Michigan State University/Feldman & Associates; 151 (cr) UCLA Fowler Museum of Cultural Arts, photograph by Don Cole; 154 (all) Superstock; 155 (tc) Ray Morsch/Corbis; 155 (tr) H. Rogers/Art Directors & TRIP Photo Library; 155 (bl) Suzanne Murphy/DDB Stock Photo; 155 (br) Alyx Kellington/DDB Stock Photo; 156 (tr) Billy Hustace/Stone; 156 (br) Paul Barton/Corbis Stock Market; 156 (cl) Kathy McLaughlin/The Image Works; 157 (tl) Richard T. Nowitz/Folio; 157 (tr) Ray Juno/Corbis Stock Market; 160 (cr) Bob Krist/PictureQuest; 160 (cl) Joe Sohm/Chromosohm/The Image Works; 161 (c) Tom & Dee Ann McCarthy/Corbis Stock Market; 161 (tr) Tony Freeman/PhotoEdit; 162 (all) The Institute of Texan Cultures

UNIT 5

Opener: (fg) Erich Lessing/Art Resource; 169 (tc) Erich Lessing/Art Resource; 170 (tl) S.A. Kraulis/Masterfile; 170 (bl) 2001 by the New York Times Co. Reprinted by permission. 1927; 170 (cr) Jon Gnass/Gnass Photo Images; 171 (bl) Paul Barton/Corbis Stock Market; 171 (cr) Science Photo Library/Photo Researchers; 175 (tl) Superstock; 175 (tr) Mark E. Gibson;175 (cl) Rommel/Masterfile; 175 (cr) Superstock; 176 (bc) PhotoDisc; 178-179 (b) Sarah H. Cotter/Bruce Coleman, Inc.; 178 (cl & cr) PhotoDisc; 179 (c, bl & br) PhotoDisc; 181 (cl) Pat Lanza/Bruce Coleman, Inc.; 184-185 (all) North Carolina

Collection, University of North Carolina Library at Chapel Hill; 186-187 (all) Kelly Culpepper; 188 (both) Historical Society of Pennsylvania; 189 (tl) Hulton/Archive; 189 (cr) Texas State Library & Archives Commission; 190-191 (t) Johnny Crawford/The Image Works; 191 (c) Kevin Horan/Stock, Boston Inc./PictureQuest; 194 (tr) Bettmann/Corbis; 196 (b) Bert Lane/Plimoth Plantation; 197 (both) Ted Curtin/Plimoth Plantation;198 (c) George F. Mobley/Courtesy U.S. Capitol Historical Society; 198 (b) Joseph Sohm/Corbis; 198 (tr) Peggy & Ronald Barnett/Corbis Stock Market; 199 (tr) Joe Sohm/Photo Researchers; 200 (t) Hulton-Deutsch Collection/Corbis; 201 (tr) United States Postal Service; 201 (br) Denise Cupen/Bruce Coleman, Inc.; 202 (c) James P. Blair/Corbis; 202 (b) Frank Siteman/Stock, Boston; 202 (tl) United States Postal Service; 202 (tr) John Neubauer/PhotoEdit; 202 (cl & cr) United States Postal Service; 203 (c) Joe Sohm/ChromoSohm Media; 203 (tr) National Archives; 208 (both) Bettman/Corbis; 209 (c) Bettman/Corbis; 209 (tr) Reuters NewMedia, Inc./Corbis; 210 (bl) Anthony Meshkinyar/Stone; 210 (br) Michael Boys/Corbis; 211 (c) H.H. Thomas/Unicorn Stock Photos; 211 (tc) Phyllis Kedl/Unicorn Stock Photos; 211 (tr) Anthony Marsland/Stone; 211 (br) Corbis; 211 (cl) PictureQuest; 212-213 (t) D. & J. Heaton/Stock, Boston; 212 (c) Chad Slattery/Stone; 212 (tl) Philip Wallick/Corbis Stock Market; 212 (bl) AFP/Corbis; 212 (br) Superstock; 213 (c) Leo de Wys Photo Agency/eStock Photography/PictureQuest; 213 (b) Torleif Svensson/Corbis Stock Market; 213 (tc) Superstock; 213 (bl) Stone; 213 (cr) Brian K. Miller/Bruce Coleman, Inc.; 214 (c) D. Young-Wolff/PhotoEdit; 214 (tl) Topham/The Image Works; 214 (tc) Archivo Iconografico, S.A./Corbis; 214 (bc) Don Mason/Corbis Stock Market; 214 (br) NASA; 214 (cl) John Elk III/Stock, Boston; 215 (c) Chris Hellier/Corbis; 215 (c) L. Hafencher/H. Armstrong Roberts; 215 (tc) Rudi Von Briel; 215 (tr) DiMaggio/Kalish/Corbis Stock Market; 216 (bl) Underwood & Underwood/Corbis; 216 (br) The Museum of Independent Telephony; 216 (cr) Corbis; 217 (tl) The Museum of Independent Telephony; 217 (tr) Superstock; 218 (bl, br, cl & cr) Thomas Neill/Old Sturbridge Village; 224 (both) Stephen F. Austin State University

UNIT 6

Opener: (fg) Smithsonian Institution; (bg) Nick Gunderson/Stone; 225 (tc) Smithsonian Institution; 226 (tl) Burke/Triolo/Brand X Pictures/PictureQuest; 226 (br) Mark E. Gibson Photography; 227 (tl) Bob Donaldson/Pittsburgh Post-Gazette; 227 (bl) David Young-Wolff/PhotoEdit; 227 (cr) Syracuse Newspaper/Katie Ciccarello/The Image Works, Inc.; 240 (b) Aneal S. Vohra/Unicorn Stock Photos; 241 (tl) Ariel Skelley/Corbis Stock Market; 241 (tr) Michael Newman/PhotoEdit; 241 (br) Christopher Bissell/Stone; 241 (bg) PhotoDisc/Getty Images; 241 (cr) Hans Reinhard/Bruce Coleman, Inc.; 242 (tl) Bob Daemmrich/The Image Works; 242 (bl) Dan Bosler/Stone; 242 (cr) Aaron Haupt/Photo Researchers, Inc.; 243 (tr) Steven Peters/Stone; 243 (cl) Richard Hutchings/Photo Researchers; 244 (b) Richard Hutchings Photography; 245 (c) Art Directors & TRIP Photo Library; 245 (cr) Bob Clay/Visuals Unlimited; 246-248 (all) Richard Hutchings Photography; 253 (c) Hans Reinhard/Bruce Coleman Collection; 254 (bl) Burke/Triolo/Brand X Pictures/PictureQuest;

254 (bc) H. Armstrong Roberts/Corbis Stock Market; 255 (tl) Spencer Grant/PhotoEdit; 255 (tr & bl) Hulton/Archive Photos; 256 (tr) Bettmann/Corbis; 256 (bl) Pittsburgh Post-Gazette; 256 (br & cl) Hulton/Archive Photos; 257 (tl) Ray Juno/Corbis Stock Market; 257 (tr) NASA; 257 (cr) Agence France Presse/Corbis; 257 (cl) Doug Martin/Photo Researchers; 258-259 (bg) Van Bucher/Photo Researchers; 262 (b) Morton Beebe, S.F./Corbis; 264 (br) Superstock; 264 (bg) Don Mason/Corbis Stock Market; 267 (cr) Anthony Meshkinyar/Stone; 268 (b) Esbian Anderson/The Image Works; 270 (b) Donnezan/Explorer/Photo Researchers, Inc.; 272 (tr) David R. Frazier; 273 (t) George Hall/Corbis; 273 (b) Stephen Kline/Bruce Coleman, Inc.; 274 (tr) Carlo Hindian/Masterfile; 274 (bl) Jef Zaruba/Corbis; 274 (br) Sven Martson/The Image Works; 275 (tl) Bob Daemmrich/Stock, Boston; 275 (tr) Rolf Bruderer/Corbis Stock Market; 275 (bl) John Lei/Stock, Boston; 275 (cl) Michael Philip Manheim/The Image Finders

All other photos from Harcourt School Photo Library and Photographers: Weronica Ankarorn, Victoria Bowen, Ken Kinzie, Quebecor World Imaging.